STUFF

YOU GOTTA KNOW

Straight Talk on Real Life

guy doud

STUFF

YOU GOTTA KNOW

Straight Talk on Real Life

CPH
SAINT LOUIS

This book is dedicated to all the youth
at Christ Community Church
in Nisswa, Minnesota,
because I thought you would like to know.

Copyright © 1993 Concordia Publishing House
3558 S. Jefferson Avenue, St. Louis, MO 63118-3968
Manufactured in the United States of America

Library of Congress Cataloging-in-Publication Data

Doud, Guy Rice, 1953–
        Stuff you gotta know : straight talk about real-life issues/Guy Rice
Doud.
        p.   cm.
        Summary: Practical advice about how God's promises relate to
such real-life issues as depression, knowing God's will, sexuality,
and alcoholism.
        ISBN 0-570-04622-X
        1. Teenagers—Religious life 2. Teenagers—Conduct of life.
        [1. Christian life. 2. Conduct of life.] I. Title. II. Title:
BV4531.2.D683 1993
248.8'2—dc20   93-25113

    2 3 4 5 6 7 8 9 10   02 01 00 99 98 97 96

Contents

When Jokes Don't Work

Why Am I Living?

Many of the jokes I've told in class are pretty corny, but most of my students are kind enough to laugh, if only to keep my feelings from being crushed. Occasionally, however, I come up with a real doozy that has students holding their sides and falling out of their desks in raucous laughter.

One day I had just finished telling a class one of my infamous jokes: *Question:* "Why did King Kong climb up the outside of the apartment building?" *Answer:* "He was too big for the elevator!"

I must admit, it certainly didn't rate as one of my real doozies. I had heard it from my son who was in kindergarten at the time, and my seniors reacted as if I had just told them a joke more suited for kindergartners. They booed and

hissed, but all in good fun. When it was all over, it was good for a hearty laugh.

But Dean didn't laugh. It seemed like he never laughed. In fact, he didn't smile. I thought about Dean for a moment, and I realized that I wasn't sure if I had ever seen him smile or laugh. He wore a perpetual frown. Why so sad?

My question was answered several days later when I went to my mailbox in the principal's office. Among my papers was a notice from the guidance office to Dean's teachers. The notice informed me that Dean was hospitalized and would be missing three to four weeks of class. On further investigation, I discovered that Dean suffered from chronic depression and was struggling with suicidal tendencies. Our school had had several student suicides over the past few years, and I prayed that Dean would get the help he needed. No one wanted to see another young life end in such a senseless way.

Dean returned to school about three weeks later. I welcomed him back and asked him how he was doing. I didn't get much more than the perfunctory "Okay." And I guess I didn't expect to get much more than that either. Dean had a wall around him that seemed quite impenetrable. As a teacher, I view such walls as a challenge, and I ask God to show me how I can get a student to "let me in." With Dean, I wrote a letter on the back of one of his essays. The letter went something like this:

Dear Dean,

I'm glad that you are back in class. I missed you when you were gone. I just want you to know that I understand depression. I have been depressed too, and have had to take prescription anti-depressant drugs. I am really glad that you went to the hospital. I want you to know that if there is anything I can do to help you, I hope you feel confident enough to know that you can ask me. Why not come in and talk sometime?

Sincerely,
Guy Doud

Several days later I was sitting at my desk after school correcting papers when I heard a knock on my door. It was Dean. I stood and said, "Come on in, Dean. Good to see ya."

He was obviously nervous, and his face was as red as a ripe tomato. Beads of perspiration stood in little balls on his forehead.

"Can we talk?" he asked, his voice shaking.

"Sure. How's it going? Is it hard coming back to school after missing three weeks?"

"Everything's hard," he said. "Life is hard. I don't fit in. Why am I living?"

10

He didn't waste any time getting to the nitty-gritty. He seemed like a time bomb, waiting to explode.

"Why do you think you're living?"

"I honestly don't know. I'm not good at anything. I can't begin to imagine what I am ever going to do for a living." Dean may have been home from the hospital, but there were obviously some very big questions for which he still needed answers.

Whenever I am in a situation like this, I ask God to make me extra sensitive. I seldom give much advice, nor do I try to set myself up as a person who has all the answers. Most of the time I try to be a good listener and to validate the feelings of the one with whom I am talking.

"You are feeling like your life doesn't matter much." It was a statement, but I made it sound more like a question.

Dean nodded his head.

I continued, "You have lots of questions about the future and you don't think very highly of yourself, do you?"

"What is there to feel good about?" I saw a flash of anger in Dean's eyes. "I'm not good at anything."

"I don't believe that for one minute. That's a lie, Dean, and you need to start telling yourself the truth." I learned a long time ago that being sympathetic often doesn't really help, but what we all need is someone who cares enough to tell us the truth.

"Okay. Tell me one thing I'm good at." The anger in Dean's voice gave way to outward defiance.

"You write good essays in my class. You are getting an A. You seem very sensitive to the needs of other people. I've noticed that you are a good listener. You are polite. You are good looking. I've seen some of the pots you've made in pottery class. You are a good potter. Should I continue?"

Dean stared at me in amazement, seemingly baffled that I knew that much about him. He didn't answer me, so I continued.

"I don't know your family, but I have a feeling that you are a very good brother and a very good son."

Tears appeared in Dean's eyes.

"As far as a career, Dean, you can do whatever you set your mind on doing. You have the intelligence and the good health to do it. You just have to stop believing all the lies you believe about yourself."

I had given far more advice than I usually like to give. I figured I should shut up and let Dean talk some more.

"In treatment they told me that I am a perfectionist and that I am too hard on myself. I have all these expectations, and when I don't meet them or when others don't meet them, I become depressed." Dean looked as if he were asking me if I agreed with the assessment.

I answered, "I've spent a good deal of my life doing the same thing, Dean. What I realized finally is that if my happiness always depends on external things over which I have no control, then I'll never be happy. You need to take your list of expectations and burn it."

There was a moment's silence, and then Dean asked, "You believe in God, don't you, Mr. Doud?"

"Yes, I do. What about you?"

"In treatment they talked about a 'higher power,' " Dean answered, "but I've always believed in God."

"If you believe in God, why do you think He made you?" I asked this rather slowly.

Dean's answer was quick in coming: "That's what I would like to know."

"And for once I think I have the answer," I said rather jokingly, but confidently.

"What is it?" Dean asked.

"You might not like it or consider it very profound, but I believe that God made you so that He could love you and help you reflect His love in your life as He empowers you to serve Him."

Dean stared at me.

I worried that my statement was too preachy, but I could tell from the look on Dean's face that he didn't take it that way.

"I've never heard that before," he said.

"I told you in the note I wrote that I have suffered from depression too. What I discovered, Dean, is that much of my depression resulted because of all those unfulfilled expectations that we were talking about. It took a loving family to help me see the truth: I was basically a pretty selfish person, who always looked at every situation and asked, 'What's in it for me?' "

I stopped for a moment before continuing. "For instance, I always wondered why no one ever called me and why I didn't seem to have any close friends. Why was I blessed with being so fat? How come I wasn't any good at math? How come I didn't have a girlfriend? Why couldn't my family have a lake cottage, as many of my friends did?"

"I've asked some of the same kinds of questions," Dean said.

"But notice in all of the questions I asked, Dean, what words appear in every one, either *I* or *my.* It was very hard for me to admit it, but I was obsessed with me. I wasn't thinking about the love God gave me in the gift of His Son or how I could serve Him. I was living to be pleased."

Dean just stared at me some more, and then he said, "I've never thought of that before."

We visited a few more minutes, and then he told me he had to get to work.

"You work at McDonald's, don't you?" I asked.

"Yes, I do."

"You don't see me in there very often. Quarter pounders are hazardous to my health!"

Dean smiled. "There was one guy who came in the other night and ate five of them."

"I used to do that, no trouble at all."

"I can't believe you used to weigh over 320 pounds."

"Believe it, Dean. Believe it. Even my fat had fat."

Another smile. A pause. "Thank you, Mr. Doud."

"Good talking with you, Dean. I hope we can do it again soon."

"Me too."

I walked him to the door and wondered, as he walked down the hall, whether my words had made any sense to him. Dean had asked a pretty basic question: "Why am I living?" And I had given him a rather unexpected answer: "Your purpose in life is to serve God and live a life pleasing to Him as He helps you to do so." The more I thought about it, I realized that there was no other answer to give.

My son Zachary will soon be three years old. He still thinks the world revolves around him. If he wants a cup of hot chocolate in the middle of the night, he doesn't think twice about waking up the entire household to let us know. Of course, one of our responsibilities is letting Zachary know that the world doesn't revolve around him. That's hard for a child to accept after spending the first few years of life getting almost everything he wants when he wants it. Wet or dirty diaper? Want it changed? Just cry loudly enough. Hungry and in need of a snack? Let your desire be known by raising your voice to 10 decibels and emitting a hair-raising scream!

I think some of us go on believing the world revolves around us, and we are forever unhappy as a result of it. I am convinced that there is a devil. His name is Satan. He specializes in telling lies. He tells us lies from the time that we are born. Here are some of his most deadly lies:

Lie: We exist so all of our desires and needs can be met.

Truth: We exist to reflect God's glory and love in all we think, do, and say.

Lie: We need to find a way to "feel good" about ourselves and have a healthy self-esteem.

Truth: We don't feel good about ourselves because we are not good. We are born with sinful natures. The Bible says clearly that our self must die. It must be crucified with Christ. When we are buried with Christ in Baptism, we are raised to newness of life. The Bible says, "Therefore, if anyone is in Christ, he is a new creation; the old has gone, the new has come!" (2 Corinthians 5:17).

Lie: Our "self-worth" is determined by how well we perform or how we look or how much money we have or how righteous we are.

Truth: We are special people (you are!) because of what Christ did on the cross. We must be very valuable to Him because He came and died for us (for you!), and our real identity is in Him. We can do nothing to earn our salvation. It is freely given to us. That's amazing grace!

These are only three of Satan's many lies, but these three alone have done more damage than can ever be measured.

Imagine how God must feel. He gave His Son for you and me so that we could be made into new people. People with new hearts, new minds, and an incredible purpose: to glorify God! We've heard the old saying that God doesn't make junk, and He doesn't! It is okay—even necessary—to not like who we are apart from God. An old hymn refers to us as worms! Imagine that! One of the best loved songs of the Christian faith is "Amazing Grace." One of the lines goes, "that saved a wretch like me."

The truth is, we are wretched without Christ, *but* when Christ lives in us He covers our wretchedness with His righteousness and our aimlessness with His purpose! If we, as God's children, feel that we are not significant or that our lives have no purpose, Satan has tricked us into failing to trust in what Christ has done for us. God's Holy Spirit leads you to the truth in His Word. Why are you living? If you are a Christian, you aren't! It is now Christ who lives in you!

I watched Dean walk through the line on graduation night to receive his diploma. I had had the opportunity to speak with him several more times. Each time we talked, I could see him becoming more and more willing to believe the idea that God did have an important plan for his life. When a board of education member handed Dean his diploma, Dean flashed a big smile.

"Now Batting for the Texas Rangers, Number 32..."

How Can I Know God's Will for My Life?

Brad was a college acquaintance of mine who was obsessed with knowing God's will for his life. First thing each morning, he would talk to God. "What do you want me to do today, Lord?" he'd ask. "Do you want me to go to class, or do you want me to go out and find someone to lead to Christ?"

According to Brad, God almost always told him to "blow off class." I wondered how come God never told me that.

I felt sorry for Brad because some of the other students thought he was crazy. Often they would scatter when he appeared. I had to admit that I thought he carried his concern about knowing God's will too far, but I wasn't ready to classify him as insane.

One day I saw Brad as he was just about to enter the cafeteria. "Hey, Brad, my man," I said, "do you want to do lunch?"

"I'll be happy to eat with you," Brad said, with no hint of approval or disapproval in his voice.

Does this guy ever lighten up? I wondered.

We grabbed our trays, and I followed Brad as we proceeded through the lunch line. Suddenly Brad stiffened, lowered his head, and stood completely still.

I knew it was unlikely, but I was afraid that he was having a heart attack. Concerned, I bent over and looked up at his bowed head and closed eyes. I noticed that his hands were folded.

The girl behind me in the lunch line asked, "Is something wrong?"

"Brad, are you okay?" I asked.

Brad nodded his head, but he didn't answer. Finally, after a few more moments of standing like that, Brad snapped to attention and said, "I am supposed to have ham and cheese on a croissant."

I was amazed. The girl behind me was amused. She laughed.

"Did you actually ask God what kind of sandwich to have?" I asked.

Stoneface said, as though expecting an argument, "We must seek God's will in all things."

"Brad, I don't really think God cares what kind of sandwiches we eat."

He looked at me as though I had committed the unpardonable sin. "God cares about every aspect of our lives. He wants us to seek His will in even the most common daily occurrences."

I said it again. "God doesn't care what kind of sandwich you eat. He just doesn't." Brad and I carried our argument to the table where we sat, and I could see that I wasn't going to get anywhere with him. He was adamant in his belief. A few days earlier I had told him that I didn't believe God wanted him to skip class all the time. He hadn't appreciated that comment either.

You will read more about Brad in chapter 12, "He Didn't Read the *Inferno* but He Found One." I can tell you, though, that Brad didn't last very long in college. He took his failure in school to be God's will too!

There is something admirable about a guy like Brad. He was very serious about his commitment to God, even though he went to extremes in attempting to interpret God's will for his life. I wondered if many of the students I met in college considered God's will at all. I've wondered, too, over the years as I've heard my high school students talk about their career objectives and goals just where, if at all, God

21

fits into their plans. I am encouraged, though, whenever I talk with teenagers at Christian youth events. One of their most commonly asked questions is "How can I know God's will for my life?"

I had just finished speaking at a Christian youth event in Phoenix, Arizona. (*Arizona readers please note:* I love being invited to speak in Arizona in January or February! By the time January rolls around I am ready for a break from the harsh Minnesota winter! If you invite me, please realize that I will have to come and stay for at least a week. It takes me the first six days just to thaw out!) My comments about God's will must have motivated the young man who was one of the first to talk to me after I finished speaking. I'll never forget his story.

"Mr. Doud," he said, "I want to play baseball."

"That was one of my dreams too," I said. (I've come to see that as rather ironic. I was a kid who couldn't even put his supporter on straight, yet I wanted to be a major leaguer!)

"I'm pretty good." Russ said it confidently without any note of arrogance.

"I bet you are," I said.

"I want to play baseball at Arizona State. My goal is to make it to the pros. I'm being recruited by a number of Division 1 schools. My coach says he thinks I have a good chance of making it to the pros." Again he displayed no

arrogance. This guy was probably even better than he would admit.

"But I've got kind of a problem."

I got a kick out of the way he said "kind of." There seems to an unwritten rule that says that if you are a guy, you don't share your problems. And even if you let on that you might be facing a serious situation, you should downplay the seriousness of it and give the impression that you really do have everything under control.

"What's the problem?" I asked.

"My dad wants me to be a minister." Russ said it as though he were asking me, What do you think?

"Ever since I was a baby he has been telling me that God was preparing me for the ministry. My dad's a pastor, and his dad was a pastor, and his dad's dad was a pastor. So I'm supposed to be a pastor."

"Wow! That puts a lot of pressure on you, doesn't it?"

"Yeah. Dad says that if I don't go into the ministry, I'll be turning my back on God's will for my life."

I looked deep into this young man's eyes and could see his pain. "You can do both, you know. You can play baseball and then go into the ministry if you feel God's leading."

"I told my dad that, but he says that it is almost impossible to be a good Christian and play professional sports. He says that I will get corrupted at a state university. He wants me to go to a Christian college."

I felt caught right in the middle. I wished I was talking with the boy's father, too, because I thought he was being extremely unfair to his son.

"You do have a problem," I said. "It sounds like your father has made up your mind for you."

"He has, but he says that God is on his side too." Now I could detect a note of anger in Russ' voice. His eyes flashed. "If it is God's will that I should be a minister and go to a Christian college, why doesn't God tell me?"

"You love your dad, don't you?" I asked.

"Of course I do; it's just that he makes me so mad sometimes. He told me that it wasn't God's will for me to go to prom this year, and it wasn't God's will for me to have a car, even though I saved up my own money to buy one. God is always speaking to my dad about me."

Kind of a problem, I thought.

"What if Dad is right? What if it is God's will for me to be a minister, and I don't want to become one? Will I be miserable my whole life?" His eyes were glued to mine now. Since my answer was slow in coming, he asked another question, "You talked about knowing God's will for your life. I guess that's what I really want to know. I want to know what is God's will, and what is my father's will."

Russ' situation was more complex than that of many young people I counsel. Still, the question was the same: How can I know God's will for my life?

I asked Russ if we could get together privately. His high school youth group was staying at the hotel for the conference. We agreed to meet at the coffee shop at 10:30 p.m. I told him to bring his Bible.

Russ was waiting for me in the coffee shop when I arrived. As I approached the booth I said, "Now pitching for the Sundevils, number 32, Russ . . ."

Russ laughed. "I'm a shortstop," he said.

"Ever take part in a triple play?"

"Came close once."

"Well, are you ready to see what the Bible has to say about God's will?"

"Yeah," Russ answered, reaching for his Bible.

Russ and I talked and read passages of Scripture until the coffee shop closed. We finished our time together sitting in the lobby of the hotel.

"I wondered about God's will for my life, too, Russ. And then an older friend of mine said that God's will is not a secret. Nor is it something that you have to agonize over trying to find. God's will is really pretty simple, and it is quite clearly laid out in His Word."

"Where in the Bible can I find whether or not I am supposed to play baseball?"

"Turn with me to the gospel according to your father, chapter 1, verse 13."

Russ laughed.

I shared with Russ that many people have some big misconceptions about God's will. They worry that if they seriously seek God's will, He will send them to Africa as a missionary, so they'd just as soon not bother finding out what His will is. I assured Russ that whatever God's will is for us, it is good and perfect. I also explained that there are some basic parts to God's will that we don't have to wonder about. God makes certain things very clear:

He wants everyone to receive the salvation He freely offers (2 Peter 3:9).

He wants everyone to enjoy the abundant life that He alone can give (John 10:10).

He wants everyone to be filled with His Spirit, so that the Holy Spirit can guide the believer in truth and bless the believer with His gifts (John 16:13–15; Galatians 5:16–25).

I asked Russ about his faith relationship with Jesus. He was a committed believer who was sure of his salvation in Christ. I shared with him that, although I believe there are definitely times when God directs a person to a particular career, most of the time, being in God's will simply means serving Him and loving Him in whatever it is that you are doing.

We read the verses in Luke that precede the story of the Good Samaritan:

> On one occasion an expert in the law stood up to test Jesus. "Teacher," he asked, "what must I do to inherit eternal life?"
>
> "What is written in the Law?" He replied. "How do you read it?"
>
> He answered: " 'Love the Lord your God with all your heart and with all your soul and with all your strength and with all your mind,' and, 'Love your neighbor as yourself.' "
>
> "You have answered correctly," Jesus replied. "Do this and you will live" (Luke 10:25–28).

"That's one of God's basics as far as I'm concerned," I told Russ. "We respond to the great love He gave to us in His Son by loving Him with all of our heart, soul, strength, and mind. And we follow Jesus' lead as we love our neighbor as much as we love ourselves. Can you love God like that and be a professional baseball player?"

"I think I could serve God best as a baseball player," Russ said. "I don't think God would have given me the talents He did if He didn't want me to use them."

"Psalm 37 contains one of my favorite verses, Russ. Look at verse 4."

"Delight yourself in the Lord and He will give you the desires of your heart."

I explained to Russ that I believe God wants us to have the desires of our hearts, as long as whatever it is we desire brings delight to Him as well.

We talked about what it means to surrender to God. I told Russ the story I had heard years ago about the man who decided that he was going to walk across Niagara Falls on a tightrope. All of his friends and neighbors told him that he was crazy and he would most surely die.

"I know I can do it," said the man.

He proceeded to set up a practice tight rope out in a field not far from his home. He practiced and practiced walking the rope the same distance he would have to walk to cross the falls. He became so good at walking the tightrope that he started pushing a wheelbarrow in front of him as he walked. After only a few short weeks he had that feat mastered too. Then he decided to add another element to his repertoire: He decided to do the stunt blindfolded. He was going to walk blindfolded across Niagara Falls while pushing a wheelbarrow!

"You will surely die," said his friends and neighbors.

"I know I can do it," said the man.

After a few more weeks of practice, the man mastered the stunt. His neighbor, who had watched him practice every day for several weeks, finally admitted, "I was one of the skeptics. I didn't think you'd be able to do it. Now I've watched you for the last several weeks, and there is no doubt in my mind whatsoever that you'll be able to succeed. I have complete faith and confidence in you! You'll do it!"

The man looked at his neighbor curiously for a moment, and then asked, "Do you really think I can do it?"

"I'm positive!" exclaimed the neighbor.

"Good," said the man. "Then why don't you ride in the wheelbarrow?"

Russ laughed. "Did he do it?"

"I don't know. I suspect not," I said. "But you know, I think a lot of people are like the neighbor. We know that God can do it! We are quick to cheer Him on from the sidelines, but then He says, 'Get in the wheelbarrow and let me give you a ride,' and all of sudden we aren't really ready to trust God anymore."

"Are you saying that I should just trust God and go into the ministry, even if I don't feel that's what is best for me?" Russ seemed terribly disappointed.

"Not at all, Russ. What I'm saying is that trusting God is a part of His will. God promises to work for our good in all that happens to us.

We can always trust Him to want what is best for us. You are facing some really big decisions right now that can affect your whole life. You're feeling as if you don't know what to do. I believe if you continue to seek the guidance of God's Holy Spirit, He will help you feel comfortable with your decision."

We turned to James, chapter 1 and read verse 5. "If any of you lacks wisdom, he should ask God, who gives generously to all without finding fault, and it will be given to him."

"What decision do you think I should make?" Russ asked.

"I'm not God," I joked. "I think you need to continue to pray, to read the Bible, and to ask the Holy Spirit for guidance and allow yourself to be open to whatever God has to say to you."

It wasn't the answer Russ expected. He wanted something more definite, I could tell.

"Then," I continued, "I think you need to sit down with your dad and your mom and tell them what it is that you feel God is leading you to do. If you can't talk with your dad, then write him a letter. Tell him that you love him and that you respect him. Tell him that it is very important for you to have his blessing on your future plans. Ask him for his blessing. Ask him to trust you to do what God is leading you to do—whatever that may be. Let him see that the decisions you've made have been made after seriously asking for God's guidance."

"What if he still says that I have to be a minister?"

"Get in the wheelbarrow, Russ. Get in the wheelbarrow. Don't worry about tomorrow. Just trust God today."

Russ and I ended our conversation in prayer. Russ prayed a beautiful prayer and told God that he really wanted to know His will. I believe Russ meant it. I prayed for better communication between Russ and his father.

Later, alone in my hotel room, I prayed again for Russ. I thought of all the other young men and women I've known who agonized to know God's will. Really, it is simple: God wants all of you. And that always leads to your becoming His servant. You may be a servant in a pulpit. You may be a servant on the baseball diamond and in the clubhouse. You may be a servant as you cut someone's hair, or you may be a servant as you change your child's dirty diaper. Wherever it is you are called to serve and whatever vehicle God gives you to drive, turn the control of that vehicle over to Him and let Him lead you one day at a time. Get in the wheelbarrow! God is true to His promises: He works faith in you through the power of the Holy Spirit and speaks to you in His Word. His Spirit will guide you and give you wisdom.

I wish I could tell you what happened with Russ, but I can't. I can tell you this, I wouldn't be surprised to tune in to a baseball game someday and hear the announcer say, "Now batting for the Texas Rangers, number 32, Russ . . ."

I wouldn't be surprised at all.

That Was Then; This Is Now

How Can I Get Along with My Parents?

Luke, my soon-to-be-nine-year-old son, could not understand why his mother and I would not allow him to wear his shorts to school last week. It was 30 degrees below zero outside and the crazy kid wanted to wear his shorts!

Understand that just a few years ago I considered shorts entirely inappropriate for school. Period. School is not the place for shorts. Mom was the one who won that victory for Luke.

"I was at his school the other day and all the other kids were wearing shorts, Guy," she said. Finally I had relented, but now I was drawing a new line. Shorts would not be worn in winter. Period. Again.

Now we were arguing about wearing shorts in the winter! I wasn't going to give in this time.

"When I went to school we couldn't even wear blue jeans!"

No one seemed to care, so I made another revelation that I thought would shock them, "And girls had to wear dresses that extended at least two inches below the knees!" Still no noticeable reaction.

"Even when it was 30 below zero outside!" Still no reaction.

"And the principal used to measure the girls' dresses with a ruler!"

"Yeah, Dad," Luke finally said, "but that was then and this is now."

With that comment my blood pressure rose about 50 points, and I felt myself getting hot under the collar. "You better watch it, young man," I said.

"Watch what?" Luke asked innocently.

"You're being a smart aleck."

"All I said was that that was then and this is now." (How dare he repeat that sarcastic remark!)

"I know what you meant!"

"What?" (More feigned innocence.)

"You know!" And I was sure that he did too.

"What?" Luke flashed a sweet smile.

I couldn't believe the next words that came out of my mouth, "When I was your age . . ." And then I stopped. What had I just said? How many times had I heard my parents say that? Hadn't I promised myself that I would never use that expression, even if I lived to be a hundred?

"Yeah, I know," said Luke, "you had to walk to school, barefoot, 25 miles, up hill both ways." Luke's smile was irresistible.

I started to laugh. "You turkey," I said. I grabbed Luke and playfully wrestled him to the ground.

He struggled loose and asked, "Well, can I wear my shorts?"

"Absolutely not. Period. End of discussion. I don't want to hear another word about it. You're not wearing shorts when it's 30 below zero outside and that's final!" Many of those words sounded strangely familiar too.

"Whhhhhhhhhhhhhhhhy?" Luke was almost whining now.

"Because I said so." I had always hated that phrase when I was a kid, but it felt good saying it as a parent. It reminded Luke, after all, who is the boss.

"Why?" Luke again. The whine was gone and he sounded angry.

"If you keep hounding me about the shorts, you're going to go to school naked!" It was a ridiculous comment and it started us both laughing again.

"Ooo, that'd be weird," Luke said, giggling.

"Now quit hounding me about the shorts. You're not wearing them. If you don't quit arguing with me about it and if you go to Mom and try to argue with her, you are going to end up being grounded for a week."

"Oh, okay." Luke accepted defeat, displeasure etched on his face, as he sharply exited and headed for his bedroom to change clothes.

Luke has been fiercely independent about the clothes he wears ever since he was a small child. He complains about everything that Tammy, his mom, picks out for him to wear. Our two-year-old, Zachary, seems to be following in Luke's footsteps. Seth and Jessica, 11 and 6 respectively, will wear whatever is laid out for them. No fuss at all. Tammy and I can't figure out how kids all raised in the same home can be so different when it comes to their tastes in what they wear.

When Luke was three, Tammy asked a question that haunts me more and more each day, "If Luke is this independent and strong-willed now, what in the world is he going to be like when he is 16?" I don't even want to think about it. I'll think about it tomorrow.

I hope it is evident that Tammy and I love Luke beyond measure. He is one of the greatest joys of our lives. Only occasionally does this type of stubborn behavior manifest itself. What this incident demonstrates is that Luke is a pretty normal kid. No doubt he thinks Dad and Mom are being unreasonable in not allowing him to wear shorts in the dead of winter. I'm sure that Luke, as well as our other three children, will believe a bunch of different things about us from time to time on their road to adulthood. I think that most kids entertain thoughts like this sometime or another:

- Mom and Dad just don't understand.
- Mom and Dad are old fashioned.
- Mom and Dad don't love me as much as they love my brother or sister.
- Mom and Dad are unreasonable and far too strict.
- Mom and Dad don't trust me.
- Mom and Dad don't like my friends.
- Mom and Dad expect too much from me.
- Mom and Dad don't give me any freedom
- Mom and Dad make me do far more work than my friends have to do.

Any of these thoughts sound familiar? I remember having most of them when I was a kid. (I can just hear Luke. "You mean back during the Ice Age?")

Well, why is it that in many (most?) families, children do not graduate from high school without at least a few major family battles being fought? And in some families it seems as though battles between parents and their children rage almost continuously. Why is this and what can be done about it?

As a parent, I have not yet had to endure the teenage years. Some of my friends who have, or have had, teenagers offer mixed assessments. One friend recently said, "My children's teenage years were the happiest years for our family. It was really fun seeing them mature and learn to make decisions for themselves."

Another friend said, "I didn't think my wife and I were going to be able to survive Tim's teenage years. It was one major battle after another. It's a miracle that we all came out alive."

Wow! Two completely different experiences. Tammy and I pray that our experience will be like the first friend's. I believe Seth, Luke, Jessica, and Zachary would like to have it that way too. So, what's the secret?

I'm convinced that there is no secret, no magic formula for family harmony and unity. In fact, the answer, I think, is well known; but the formula is often ignored. Family unity doesn't occur by chance. It takes teamwork, patience, forgiveness, perseverance (that means you stick to it!) and a whole lot of love.

Most important, families can be led by God's Spirit to follow the principles that He established for families in His Word. The wife is to be subject to the husband as the spiritual leader in the family. The husband demonstrates that leadership by loving his wife and children as Jesus loves him. The husband treats his wife as a gift from God. Children are to honor their parents. Parents are to love their children and care for them as special gifts from God. All members of the family are subject to God, following His desires and obeying His commands.

I think many Christian couples get married, intending to practice the biblical formula for the family, but the good intentions don't give way to action. Consequently, family functions and responsibilities are left to chance. That's like throwing seed to the wind and hoping that somewhere a crop grows.

Someone has said that it is strange that to drive a car you must get a license by demonstrating a certain proficiency at driving, but no license is required to bear children and no proficiency need be demonstrated before becoming a parent. So what model do parents follow as they begin the journey of parenthood? Usually parents end up parenting in the way they were parented. Unless the home from which they came functioned very well, the home they establish may be filled with the same problems they experienced in childhood.

Understanding this helped me understand my parents, and understanding is a key to effective communication. It may startle you for me to admit it, but sometimes parents are too strict. Sometimes parents are unfair. Sometimes parents are insensitive. Sometimes parents are old fashioned. They, too, are sinful.

You may not like to hear this, but your God-given responsibility as a son or daughter is to honor your parents and obey them. Don't turn me off! Read on, because I think some of the rest of what I have to share may help you understand your parents and may help you open the lines of communication so that you can have a more harmonious relationship.

A few months ago, Seth, age 11, walked into my bathroom as I was shaving. "Dad," he asked, "can I use some of your cologne?"

"What for?" I asked. (Then I realized how stupid the question was. What did I think he was going to do with it? Drink it?)

"I want to smell good," he said, somewhat embarrassed.

Then I remembered that this was the same kid who had had numerous crushes on numerous girls ever since first grade. (I had a hard time relating to Seth's infatuations. I don't think I even knew girls existed until high school, and then I was so frightened of them, I blushed whenever I saw one.) Seth was the same kid who asked for money in third grade so he could send a girl some roses! Now here he stood, my baby, asking for my cologne!

Parents have this thing—it's very hard for us to admit that our children are growing up. When we face that fact, we have to contend with some related facts:

I'm growing older too! That's very hard to admit. You see, I'm almost 40 and I still think of myself as a teenager.

Soon the kids will be dating. No girl is good enough for my son! No boy is good enough for my daughter! And what if they . . . you know? I don't want to think about it! I'll think about it tomorrow.

They'll be leaving home soon and they won't need me anymore. As strange as this sounds, parents receive a sense of satisfaction from knowing they can meet their children's needs. It feels good to be needed. Sometimes it is hard to adjust to your "baby" telling you, "I can do it myself, Dad, thanks anyway."

I wish I would have . . . When parents realize their children are growing up, they sometimes feel guilty about all the things they wish they had done differently. The guilt may be over seemingly minor things: "I wish I would have videotaped her more when she was a baby." Or a parent may feel guilty about more serious problems: "I was hardly home while he was growing up. I didn't make it to many of his school programs. I wish I had played more with him. Now he would rather spend more time with his friends than with me."

That's some pretty major guilt. The strange thing is that parents don't always know how to deal with their guilt. Rather than confess it and ask God and their children for forgiveness, they try to stuff it down inside. That doesn't work. Guilt will usually manifest itself in some way. One way it rears its ugly head is in anger. And guess who is often the victim of the anger? Strange, isn't it, that we often get angry at the ones we love the most?

These are only a few of the thoughts parents face when they realize that their children are growing up. In chapter 4, I offer further insight into some parents' behavior when I answer this question: Why don't my parents care about each other and about me?

I remember one recent argument I had with Seth and Luke. They wanted to go over to a friend's house. Without much thought, I said no.

"Why?" was their logical question.

"I want you to stay home," was my answer. That obviously didn't satisfy their demand to know why I had said no. Actually, I wasn't exactly sure why I said no at the time. Sometimes I think parents say no just because it is a natural instinct. The more I thought about my reason for saying no this time, however, I realized it was because I enjoyed their company and wanted to spend some time with them. I had been traveling for a few days. When I am away from my family, I get lonely. I hadn't seen much of the kids since I got home, and I wanted to spend some time with them.

It may be hard for you to believe, but no one on this earth loves you more than your parents. Sometimes they really just enjoy your company. I make this statement realizing that some children are abandoned or abused by their parents. If this has happened to you, I realize your heartache and am not insensitive to your pain. I address your circumstance in another chapter. Here, however, I'm discussing the average family, and most parents would gladly give their lives for their children. It may be deep in your parents' subconscious mind, but I think at times a still, small voice speaks to your mom and dad and says, "Jennifer is growing up, you know. Soon she'll be out of the house and on her own, you know. You won't see much of her then, you know. She'll be even more independent than she is now." (All the "you knows" suggest that that still, small voice is of Scandinavian ancestry.)

At that very moment Jennifer walks up to her mom and asks, "Can I go to Julie's party?"

Mom's answer is immediate, "No." And she has said no before she even realizes she has said it. Understanding this may help you to understand your parents just a bit better. With that understanding comes better communication and a deeper respect for one another's point of view.

You may be saying, "Wait a minute, Guy! Why do I always have to be the one who understands? What about my parents trying to understand my point of view?"

Good point, and I think they should. Understanding and communication are two-way streets. But the bottom line is this: You are to obey your parents, even if they are unreasonable.

Sometimes your parents see the big picture that you don't see. For instance, Zachary, our soon-to-be-three-year-old, can't understand why he has to wait for Christmas to open his packages. He wants to open them now. He isn't unlike most kids in that respect. In fact, one of the major differences between mature people and immature people is the ability of mature people to delay gratification. Children want all their needs met immediately. Mature people realize that sometimes meeting a perceived need, while enjoyable in the short term, may actually be harmful in the long run.

Another example: You are five and your uncle gives you a bag of candy. You try a few pieces and decide to eat the whole bag. Your mom takes the bag away from you because she doesn't want you to spoil your supper. Also, she doesn't want you to eat all that sugar or all those calories. You think, Mom is unreasonable. This scenario usually occurs with small children, but the concept is the same as a child gets older. Just the circumstances change.

A 15-year-old may think that Dad and Mom are being unreasonable (and sometimes maybe they are), but more than likely the parents do know what is best for their children and are watching out for their best interests. It is hard to explain this to a teenager who thinks Mom and Dad make their decisions arbitrarily. When I was a kid I sometimes thought that my parents made their decisions based on one criteria—what would aggravate me the most! I look back now and realize that they saved me from a lot of bad choices. I'm thankful that they didn't always let me have my way.

It is a hard teaching, but you must accept your parents' authority over you. Show them that you respect them and the decisions they make. Earn their trust by showing them that you can be trusted. In many families a number of circumstances seem to cause the most problems:

How you talk and treat one another. Everyone wants to be treated with respect. As God's beloved children, you deserve your parents' respect and they deserve yours. You'll get along better if you speak politely to one another. Make eye contact with your parents when they are talking to you. Try not to interrupt. Wait for your chance to speak. If your chance doesn't come, kindly ask permission. Following this strategy will prevent lots of arguments.

How much work you do around the house. I've discovered that many family arguments occur over things that really aren't that "big": Who left the door open? Whose turn is it to take out the garbage? Most of these arguments can be avoided if the family defines a clear division of labor and everyone understands what is expected of him or her. One helpful rule: All family members who are capable should pick up after themselves. Bedrooms often become battle zones when beds are not made and clothes are not picked up.

Try this plan: Keep your bed made and your room clean. Take out the garbage without being asked. Volunteer to do the dishes. If you see the milk sitting out or the door open, don't worry about who left it sitting out or who failed to shut it, just put the milk away and shut the door. (Think about all the times that Mom and Dad changed your diaper. They weren't the ones who dirtied it, were they?) If you start acting in this way, you might be surprised at how your parents respond. Acting in a loving and kind fashion is like throwing water on a fire.

Reacting argumentatively is like spraying the fire with gasoline.

How you dress and wear your hair. Your parents feel that you are a direct reflection of themselves. They believe that if someone sees you dressed in shorts when it is 30 below outside, they'll think, Oh my, Guy and Tammy Doud must not care about their kids.

Sometimes parents need to be known as parents who have their family "under control" competes with your need for self-expression. In a healthy family there is room for compromise. Consider this factor: How can I best dress and groom myself to bring honor and glory to God? As we grow up, we tend to want to express our individuality. Sometimes this leads us to dress in a way or wear our hair in a way that shocks our parents. I believe it is important that our dress and hairstyle meet with our parents' approval. It is most important to remember that the way we dress can affect our witness for God.

How you value money. Concern over money seems to be at the root of many problems. I was amazed at the "wish list" my kids assembled last Christmas. Zachary sat with the "wish book" and pointed to almost every toy on every page. "I want this. I want this. Look at this. I want it." It was cute because he was only two and I knew that he wouldn't be upset if he didn't get all that he wanted. He was still at the age when he was happy with whatever he got.

Obviously, Zachary doesn't have any concept of money. I'm not sure our older kids do, either. I realize that it is the parents' responsibility to instill in their children a proper respect for money. Many times parents leave this responsibility to chance, and then when their children don't seem to value money as they (the parents) do, conflict occurs. Parents teach most effectively by example. Unfortunately, many kids know nothing about the family budget or their parents' priorities. Regrettably, some young people see their parents make unwise financial decisions, like piling up credit-card debt. Then when a parent corrects a child, the child points a finger back at the parent. "Why don't you practice what you preach?" is the obvious question.

My experience as a high school teacher would suggest to me that many of the teenagers I've taught don't have their priorities in order when it comes to spending money. Why do I say that? I don't know how many times I've witnessed my students—who are worried about having enough money to go to college—buying elaborate CD equipment or leather coats or expensive shoes that I wouldn't even consider buying for myself.

I remember one conversation I had with a student who was flunking out of my class. "Well, Phil," I said, "you miss a lot of class time, and when you are here, you can barely stay awake."

"Yeah, I know," Phil answered. "I work late and I don't get much sleep."

"Maybe you should quit work," I suggested.

Phil's eyes opened wide at my suggestion. "No. I have to work so I can pay for my car."

"Why do you need a car?" I asked.

He looked at me as though I were a complete idiot before he answered me, "I have to have the car so I can get to work."

Now, maybe I am old fashioned, but I think that school should be a young person's highest priority after commitment to God and family. This is another area where major battles break out in the home. Phil placed making money ahead of school. He placed having a car ahead of school. Misplaced priorities often cause conflicts between teenagers and their parents.

One parent told me recently, "My son and daughter are both in college. They want to have everything I have, and they want it right now. What they don't realize is that I have had to work all my life to get what I've got."

Much conflict will be avoided in the family if all family members see money as the means to acquire essentials, rather than as the essential thing to be acquired.

These are just a few of the areas where trouble breaks out in the family. Trying to understand your parents' point of view and remembering God's design for families will do much to help you get along with your parents. Ask God to help you and your parents get along. God works powerfully in answer to prayer. Give this book to your parents. Ask them to read this chapter and tell you what they think of it. Open a dialog with your parents and talk with them about the things that are on your heart. With God's help and guidance, family harmony is possible as you learn to listen to one another, celebrate God's forgiveness for the times you fail, forgive one another, and follow His plan for your family.

You know what? I just got back from a fast-food restaurant where I went for lunch. Today it is only eight above outside. You know what I saw at that restaurant? There were a whole bunch of kids—about Luke's age—wearing shorts! Can you believe it?

"And Miles to Go before I Sleep"

Why Don't My Parents Care about Each Other and Me ?

Jake had been to my room many times after school. Sometimes he stopped by just to chat. He always wore a smile and seemed the eternal optimist. Sometimes he came at my invitation, given out of my concern that he pass my class. Each time Jake came to my room I encouraged him to do his school work and tried to offer help. But my offers went unheeded and his grade in American literature continued to slide. Unless something dramatic happened, it appeared that he was going to fail the class for the second time.

I knew that time was running out for Jake. A high school senior, he should have passed American literature during his junior year. Now here it was the final quarter of his senior year, and he still had a long way to go to receive a passing grade. One recent assignment was to memorize Robert Frost's famous poem "Stopping by Woods on a Snowy Evening." For one test they were to write out the poem's four stanzas and to provide an analysis. Most students did a pretty good job remembering the poem, as we had recited it together at the beginning of class for several weeks. Jake, however, could only remember the poem's last two lines. He wrote, "And miles to go before I sleep, And miles to go before I sleep."

Beneath *sleep* I wrote, "Jake, please come and see me."

Jake was smiling as usual as he entered my room that Friday, not long after the bell signaled the end of the school week. (Teachers are no different than students. We look forward to weekends too.) I was packing some essay tests into my briefcase—my homework for the weekend—when Jake walked into the room and sat in his customary chair, right in front of my desk. I figured he had come to talk about Robert Frost.

"Well, I've been kicked out of my house," Jake said matter of factly, as though it were something that happened every day.

At first I thought he was joking. "What do you mean you've been kicked out?" I wondered how any parent could kick a child out of the house. I remembered how my mother used to

threaten to send my brother Patrick and me to reform school in Red Wing, Minnesota. But we knew it was something of a joke. I couldn't conceive of getting kicked out on the street.

"Ever since my parents' divorce last October, Mom has been saying that if I don't shape up, she wants me to go live with my dad."

"Oh, so you're moving in with your father then?" That seemed reasonable enough.

"No," Jake said. "He doesn't want me either. He's living with his girlfriend and I think he thinks I'd be in the way."

"Jake, I don't understand." And I didn't.

"I don't either," Jake said, trying to make a joke of it.

"No, what I mean is, I don't understand how a parent can just throw a child out of the house. Parents have a legal obligation and responsibility."

"I'm almost 19," Jake said. "I've failed a few grades. Mom said that she wants to sell the house and move out to California. She doesn't want me to tag along. She says she wants her freedom."

Jake paused for a minute. "Mom and I, we don't get along too good. We always argue. She hangs out at the bar until closing time, and then she comes home and starts ragging on me. Last night we had a big argument. I was supposed to have washed the clothes, and I didn't get them done. So we started arguing and she said she just couldn't take it anymore and kicked me out."

"She kicked you out last night?" I asked.

"Yeah."

"Where did you sleep?"

"In my car."

"Have you talked to your mom today?"

"No. She said she doesn't want to talk to me anymore." Jake's eyes seemed to search mine for some word of hope.

I tried, "Well, maybe she has calmed down since last night. I bet that when you go home now things will have blown over."

"I don't think so," Jake said. He gave a brief smile that indicated he knew more about it than I did.

"Why don't you think so?"

"Mom packed all my clothes and put them in my car along with a note. I found them at lunch time. The note said that she was having the lock changed on the house and that I shouldn't call her, she'll call me."

"I can't believe this," I said.

"I know, I can't believe it either."

"Are you sure your father won't help you out?" Even though his father was living with someone, I figured Jake would be better off living with him than living in his car.

"Well, you see, he's not my real father."

I wondered how much more complex the story could get. "Where is your real father?" I asked.

"I don't know," Jake confessed. "I've never known him. Mom said that he dumped her when he found out she was pregnant. Last she knew, she thought he was going to Alaska."

As details of Jake's personal life and family history continued to unfold, I started to feel a little guilty. I had been just "doing my job" when I expected him to fulfill the requirements of my American literature class. But I could see now that what this young man really required was not a knowledge of Thoreau or Emerson or Frost: He needed to know that he was loved.

"What are you going to do?" I asked.

"I don't know. I suppose I can sleep in my car again."

"That isn't a solution," I said, wondering what the solution was. None of my education classes in college had prepared me for this moment or for many of the moments I routinely encounter as a teacher.

I thought about the trailer house where Tammy and I lived. We already had a renter in the one extra bedroom, and I knew that there wasn't any room for Jake.

I called Social Services, hoping that they would be able to help. I thought Jake could be placed in a foster home. But since Jake was a legal adult, he wasn't eligible for a foster home. The more I talked with Social Services, the more I became aware of all the complex legalities. No help was available without having to fill out thousands of forms and wait for days and weeks.

Finally, I called a friend from church. "Pam, I need to talk with you a minute." I explained the situation to Pam, and as expected, after checking with her husband, she was willing to have Jake come and stay at her home. Both of her children had gone away to college, so she had the room. I also knew that Pam and her husband would show Christ's love to Jake.

My teaching experiences have shown me that there are many young people like Jake. Maybe they aren't literally kicked out of the house, but they feel abandoned by their parents, nevertheless. Varying circumstances can cause feelings of abandonment.

Jake was abandoned by his biological father. That is happening with more and more frequency. Many women today even plan to have children out of wedlock, knowing that the father may not wish to have anything to do with the child. As with Jake's father, many young men shirk the responsibility of parenthood and never have any involvement with the children they father. Even if the mother is loving and caring, committed to raising the child in a good home, a child may feel that he or she has been deprived of a father.

I remember visiting with a young girl who, like Jake, had never known her father. He had died when she was very young. She, too, felt abandoned. She had not recognized her feelings as feelings of abandonment. But after visiting with me for a while, she realized that not only did she feel abandoned, she was angry at her father for not being there for her as she grew up. Even though her father's death wasn't his fault (he had been killed by a drunken driver), she couldn't deny that she felt abandoned and angry. Once she recognized these feelings, she could work through them.

Some of us feel abandoned if a parent puts work ahead of us. I'll never forget the look in my son's eyes when I broke a promise I had made to him to take him to a Minnesota Twins baseball game. Why did I break my promise? I had a good excuse: I had to work. Even though I could rationalize and justify my need to fulfill my work obligation, my son, understandably and rightly so, still felt like I had put work before him. Parents whose jobs require them to be absent from the home for long periods of time may not realize that, not only do their children feel abandoned, but their spouse may very well feel abandoned too.

More children are abandoned through divorce than through any other means. Almost 50 percent of all adults get divorced. Studies show that divorce significantly changes the relationship between a child and his or her father. Even though the father may be well intentioned, it is difficult for divorced fathers whose ex-wives have custody of the children to maintain meaningful contact with the children.

Jake was abandoned by his biological father before he was born. He was abandoned by his mother and his stepfather at the age of 18. No doubt he'd felt abandoned emotionally many years earlier. The truth is—Jake was an abused child. No, he wasn't physically beaten or sexually molested. But as I listened to his story, I realized that he had been neglected for most of his life. He had been deprived of the love and nurture that he should have received from the moment he was conceived. This type of passive abuse can be just as damaging as overt physical or sexual abuse.

Why do some parents fail to care for their children? Why do some parents fail to care for one another? Sometimes parents may be under a lot of stress that their children are not aware of. They may experience stress at work, or they may experience financial problems. There may even be problems in your parents' relationship that they have tried to hide from you. This tension may prevent you from experiencing the depth of attention and love you feel you need.

Sometimes, lack of care and concern presents a much deeper problem than you can even begin to conceive. Some people do not know how to love or to receive love. Father Martin, a Catholic priest who has had a wonderful ministry to alcoholics and their loved ones, tells a wonderful story that illustrates well the point I'm trying to establish.

A man went to his doctor. "Doctor," the man said, "I'm dead."

"Nonsense," said the doctor, checking the man's pulse, temperature, and blood pressure, "you're very much alive."

The man insisted, "No, Doctor, I know I'm dead."

The doctor wanted to bring an end to this ridiculous discussion, so he asked the man a question, "Okay, John, let me ask you a question. Do dead men bleed?"

John answered immediately, "Of course not, Doctor. Everyone knows that dead men don't bleed."

"Good," the doctor said. "I'm glad we agree on that. Give me your finger, John."

John raised his hand and the doctor grabbed it. "What are you going to do, Doc?"

The doctor answered by taking a pin and poking John's finger. John stared as the red blood came flowing out. "Well, what do you say now, John?" the doctor asked.

"I can't believe it, Doctor," exclaimed John. "Dead men do bleed!"

You see, John was so convinced that he was dead that, despite the doctor's graphic evidence otherwise, he wasn't about to change his mind. Now what does this have to do with parents not loving their children or not loving each other? It is difficult to change a belief that is built upon a lifetime of learning. Your parents may have grown up feeling unloved and abandoned too. Maybe your father doesn't know how to express love toward you or how to share his feelings because his father never set the example for him. Maybe your mother is obsessed with being a perfectionist and wants you to be perfect, too, because it is part of a cycle that goes all the way back to your great-grandparents.

I've met many young people who feel frustrated because their parents have set such high expectations for them. I was visiting with a girl recently who had studied ballet since she could walk. She is now a junior in college. She is very accomplished, but she admitted to me that she really didn't like ballet. Her exact words, "I'm a ballerina because my mother always wanted to be a ballerina." Parents often live out their unfulfilled dreams through the lives of their children. This is tremendously unfair to the children, and parents sometimes don't realize what they are doing.

There are many possible explanations for the way Jake's mother treated him. I can't say why she was unable to give him the love he needed. Pam and I tried to help Jake understand that it wasn't his fault, that he was not unlovable. Jake's mother needed love as much as he did. Perhaps she didn't have any love to give because she had never received any love.

The sin of an individual can damage those around him or her even if the others are innocent of that sin. Is it any surprise, then, that in families where one of the parents is an alcoholic, the chances of children developing alcoholism rise substantially? that a child who has been physically or sexually abused may grow up to be an abuser?

A child may think that a parent doesn't care, when actually the parent cares very much. How can this be? The parent's perception of reality might be as confused as John's— "Dead men do bleed." A parent might feel she is sharing love freely, but in reality, her relationship with her child does not seem loving at all. Modern-day psychology uses lots of terms to label adults with relationship problems. They may be "adult children" of alcoholic parents or "codependents" or "workaholics" or any number of other things.

Exploring Jake's background further, we discover that his mother's parents had been divorced and his mother's mother had had a child out of wedlock. Adults tend to recreate the childhood home in which they were raised. There seems to be an almost natural instinct to want to recreate one's family of origin. Even though that family may have been troubled, the old patterns and relationships have become a part of the adult's behavior and perception.

Does a troubled background absolve parents of their responsibility? Absolutely not. The past may offer an explanation as to why someone has certain beliefs or behaves in a certain way, but ultimately we must all take responsibility for our own lives. If we do come from homes like Jake's, we need God's help to break the cycle so that we do not pass the same problems on to our children and to our children's children.

I remember explaining all of this once to a girl who was feeling unloved by her parents. She had built up a tremendous amount of resentment and anger toward both her mother and father. I encouraged her to "walk a mile in her parents' shoes." I asked her some questions about her mother's family and her father's family. She started to see that what was happening in her family was part of an ongoing cycle. Although she rightfully did not absolve her parents of their responsibility, she suddenly felt compassion for them, and her resentment turned to understanding and then forgiveness I'll never forget her comment, "I suddenly realize that my mother needs love—as much love as I do."

How can the cycle be broken? It depends on how serious the situation is. If your family is struggling to care for one another and there is a lack of love shown between your family members, try to assess the situation. What is causing the problem? Sometimes problems occur because family members have taken their eyes off God and focused on themselves. If you think your family might have this problem, ask your parents to sit down and pray with you. Read God's Word together and focus on the great love God shares with us in Jesus. Ask His help in sharing that love. If, with God's help, parents recommit themselves to living out their marriage vows and parents and children recommit themselves to one another in the way God intends, many problems will soon disappear.

If your family is suffering from severe problems, professional counseling may be needed. If you are in an abusive situation and are afraid to talk with your parents, talk to your pastor or a teacher you trust right away.

God did not entrust you into the care of your parents so they could abuse you. Focus on Jesus Christ and His great love for you. Jesus will never abandon you. He always has time for you. His love and grace are sufficient for you. He alone is able to fill empty hearts.

Jake lived with Pam and her husband the last couple of months of his senior year. Then he enlisted in the Navy and off he went. Whenever he was home on leave he would drop by the high school to see me. Once when I wasn't at school, he called me at home. I had the feeling that he thought he had to report in to me. I appreciated it too. By the way, Jake did pass American literature. I forgot to tell you that, in addition to being a fine Christian lady, Pam was an English major. I suspect she helped Jake with his studies. I think she also told him about Jesus!

I haven't seen or talked with Jake for several years now. The last time I saw him, it was obvious to me that he was a survivor—despite a less-than-happy childhood. He told me he loved the Lord and that made me feel real good. I remember him standing outside the door of my room. "Are you going to reenlist," I asked.

"Yes, sir," he said.

"Good," I said, "I'm glad to know that our country is being served by guys like you, Jake."

"Thank you, Mr. Doud," he said, blushing from my compliment. And then he said, "Well, I guess I'd better get going. I've got 'miles to go before I sleep, And miles to go before I sleep.' "

There Is a Twinkle in His Eye Again

Someone I Love Is an Alcoholic.
What Do I Do?

"Hi. I'm Cindy and I'm an alcoholic."

"Hi, Cindy."

If you've ever been to a meeting of Alcoholics Anonymous, you recognize that dialog. I'll never forget the first AA meeting I attended. I sat rather stunned as all these people, young and old, stated their names and then said, "I'm an alcoholic." I was attending a training school on chemical dependency, and part of the training involved attending an open AA meeting. I was learning a lot about alcoholism. One thing I learned was that alcoholism is, in one sense, a disease and that it is no respecter of persons. In other words, it doesn't matter how much money one has, how "religious" one is, how intelligent one is, or how well-liked or popular one is, everyone is a potential victim of the dis-

ease of alcoholism. Anyone who drinks with some regularity stands the risk of becoming addicted. Addiction means that the body craves the addictive substance, in this case, alcohol. If one is raised in a family where a parent is addicted, one's chances of becoming addicted rise substantially.

Becky was in one of my discussion classes and was also a member of the student council that I advised. She was a bright girl with a bright smile. In my discussion classes I always try to create an atmosphere where students feel comfortable enough to share. I've witnessed some unbelievable scenes. I'll never forget the day that Kent Soderman, a young man dying of brain cancer, answered questions from the class about whether or not he was afraid to die. And I'll never forget the day when a panel of students made what I thought was going to be a routine presentation on alcoholism. Becky was a part of that panel.

Each student on the panel presented a different topic regarding alcoholism. One student informed the class of current treatment procedures. One panel member covered the controversy concerning defining alcoholism as a disease and how some people want to define it as a moral weakness. This student commented: "Some people say that if alcoholism is a disease, then it is the only disease that comes in a bottle." Yet another panel member reported on support groups associated with alcoholism—Alcoholics Anonymous, Al-Anon, and Alateen. The kids were listening that day, but they really got interested when it was Becky's turn to speak.

"Hi," she said, "I'm Becky, and my dad is an alcoholic." Then Becky shared her story. Her father, a successful businessman, had almost destroyed his entire family, his business, and his health with his drinking. Still, he failed to admit that he had a problem. Becky told us that this type of denial is one of the symptoms of alcoholism. She also said that alcoholics try to rationalize, or make excuses, for their drinking. They try to minimize the effects of their drinking with comments like this: "I don't drink as much as my friend." "The reason I got a little drunk last night was because I was stressed out from work. I just needed to let my hair down."

Becky told us about how she and her mom had tried to get her father to stop drinking. They threatened to move out. They begged him. He would improve for a little while and make lots of promises, but he never kept them. "That was the hardest thing for me to understand," Becky said. "My dad wanted to keep his promises, but he couldn't. He was addicted.

"I've grown up watching my father pass out in his chair in front of the television almost every night." Tears came to Becky's eyes. The class grew uncomfortable.

"Becky," I said, "I want to thank you for sharing. Class, in AA or Alateen, whatever you share in the group meeting is not to be discussed elsewhere. I ask you to please respect Becky's privacy and the privacy of her family."

The class was strangely silent.

"Becky," I asked, "do you and your mom attend any support groups?"

"Yes," Becky answered, "I go to Alateen and Mom goes to Al Anon."

"Would you mind explaining to the class what those groups are for?" I asked.

"No. When someone you love is an alcoholic you become almost as sick as that person. You often lie about their behavior because you are ashamed. You try to cover for them. You make excuses for them. You may tend to blame yourself and think that you are the reason for the drinking. Your whole view of life gets out of whack if someone you love a lot is an alcoholic. My mom says that although she doesn't drink, Dad's booze makes her deluded too—that means she can't think straight and see things as they really are. That's why we go to support groups, to help us to see things the way they really are and to help keep us from enabling Dad."

"That's a wonderful explanation, Becky, thank you," I said. I paused a moment. The class was still very quiet. I continued, "Both of my parents were alcoholics. Both stopped drinking and went to AA. Anyone else in here have a loved one who is an alcoholic?"

Four or five hands went up among the 30 students in class.

"That's pretty typical," I said. "According to statistics, one out of every ten Americans is an alcoholic."

"How do you know if someone is an alcoholic?" one boy asked.

"Well, does anyone care to answer that?" I directed the question at the panel.

Doug, who had presented information on current treatment procedures, was prepared to answer. He handed out a sheet of paper that explained the four stages of alcoholism. He explained the handout: "In stage 1 you learn that alcohol changes your mood. It usually makes you feel euphoric—your troubles don't bother you. And since you usually drink your first drinks or beers with friends, drinking is associated with a good time."

"So is everyone who has ever had a drink in the first stage of alcoholism?" The boy who asked the question sounded somewhat cynical.

I loved the answer that Doug gave, "I don't know. I guess so." And then he continued:

"Stage 2 is when the person who has learned about the mood swing begins to look for opportunities to drink. At this stage, alcohol becomes more than just something you might have once in a while. It is something that you plan on having; you see it as essential in order to have a good time."

I was amazed at how well-prepared Doug was. I realized that alcohol and alcoholism were topics that my students were far more familiar with than most topics we discussed.

Doug continued, "At stage 3 the drinker no longer just looks for opportunities to drink, but becomes obsessed with drinking. He begins to plan his life around drinking. Drinking is beginning to cause many problems, but the alcoholic keeps right on drinking. This stage, my health teacher said, is harmful dependency. The drinker is very unlikely to stop drinking at this stage unless someone intervenes."

And then Doug looked up from his notes and said, "That's what we had to do with my dad." Doug was no longer reading from his notes, he was talking from his heart. "My dad's boss and Mom and my two sisters and I held an intervention. That's where you try to get the alcoholic to see himself as he really is. My dad's boss told Dad that unless he went to treatment, he was going to be out of a job. Mom and my sisters and I told him that unless he went to treatment, we couldn't live with him any-more."

Doug paused. I asked the question that was on everyone's lips: "Did your father agree to go to treatment?"

"Yes, he did," Doug answered. "He said he never realized that his drinking was hurting so many people."

"How is your dad doing now, Doug?"

"He's been sober for three years."

"That's wonderful," I said. (Although I wanted to say, "Praise the Lord!")

A smile came over Doug's usually somber face. "My dad is an entirely different guy now that he doesn't drink anymore."

I looked over at Becky. How I knew she wished the same for her father.

One of the guys from the back of the room asked, "What is stage 4?"

"Stage 4 is when the alcoholic no longer drinks to feel euphoric or high," Doug explained. "In this stage the goal of drinking is just to try to feel normal."

"Doug," I said, "you did an excellent job explaining the four stages of alcoholism. When I trained at a place called the Johnson Institute I heard something I'll never forget. One old guy had been sober for 20 years but still referred to himself as a 'drunk.' He looked at our group and asked, 'Want to know what an alcoholic is?

I'll tell ya what an alcoholic is. Tell someone to go without alcohol for three months, and if the thought of that frightens him, tell him he's an alcoholic. If alcohol is causing problems in your life and you continue to use it, you're an alcoholic.' The facilitator of our class said he thought that was one of the best definitions of alcoholism he had ever heard, and I've never forgotten it."

The panel finished its summary statements just as the bell rang to end the class. I stood at the door and said good-bye to the students as they left. I complimented the panel members on the fine job they had done. As Becky passed by, our eyes met and I said, "I'll be thinking about you and your family. I'll be praying for you."

"Thank you," she said.

Most of the students had left, but one girl lingered behind. "Mr. Doud," she said, "I think one of my best friends is an alcoholic. What should I do?"

"What kind of problems is the drinking causing in her life?" I asked.

"She's skipping school to go drinking. Her grades are suffering. She hardly bothers to eat anymore. She does stupid things like shoplifting. And she doesn't seem to want to have anything to do with her old friends, unless they go along with what she is doing. She's mad at me because I told her that I think she has a drinking problem."

"Good for you," I said.

"What can I do?" She was genuinely concerned.

"You've already started helping her by telling her the truth about her drinking. Who else have you talked to?"

"Some of her other friends. We're all concerned."

"Are her parents aware of the extent of her drinking?" I asked.

"Her mom and dad got divorced last year and she took it really hard. It seems like her mom lets her do whatever she wants now because she feels so guilty about the divorce."

"So you don't think her parents know how much she is drinking and what kind of problems it's causing?"

"I can't see how they can't know, but it's like they don't want to see it."

"Is your friend still in school?" I asked.

"When she comes."

"I think we need to get involved in your friend's life before she kills herself. I know you're concerned about harming your friendship, but if you really care for her, you must be willing to risk it. The alternative could mean death."

"What can I do?"

"Let's go see her counselor. If your friend's attendance and grades are as bad as you say they are, then that's a lot of proof right there that something is wrong. I think the counselor will need to talk to her parents and perhaps to some of your friend's other friends and figure out the best way to get her the help she needs."

I saw both hope and fear in her eyes.

"You're doing the right thing," I said. "It takes courage, but you could help save her life."

I walked the student down to the guidance office, found the appropriate counselor, and made the referral. I was pleased with the courage this girl had shown.

One of the most frustrating things about teaching is that you become absorbed in lives of kids for as many as three years. You learn about them and their struggles and their joys, and then they are gone and you lose touch with most of them. A few keep in touch for a few years; some I'll be in touch with forever, I imagine. But most of the students leave high school, and I lose complete touch with them within a few short years. I will never know how some of their lives turn out. Did Becky's father ever quit drinking? Did Doug's father remain sober? How many students who sat in my classroom the day of the panel discussion on alcoholism— how many of them became alcoholics? Did anything I taught them make a lasting impression? I always wonder.

I hope the students who were in my discussion that day learned that alcoholism is treatable, even though it is marked by denial and rationalization. Those who love the alcoholic must tell the truth about the condition. Those who love the alcoholic must get help for themselves because the disease affects them too. There are many resources available. School counselors, pastors, hospital programs, local chapters of Alcoholics Anonymous and Al-Anon and Alateen can all offer support and suggestions for helping a friend or a loved one who is an alcoholic.

There is one key point I don't think anyone made in my discussion class that day: If you suspect that someone you love is an alcoholic, seek help immediately. The sooner alcoholism is arrested the better. Even if the alcoholic chooses to keep drinking, the sooner *you* receive help, the better.

There is something else I wish I could have told the class: God cares deeply about the addicted person and those close to him or her. God is able to provide strength, healing, wisdom, and new life. In treatment and in AA and other support meetings, those who use the 12 steps of Alcoholics Anonymous refer to a "higher power." For the Christian, that higher power is not anonymous. We know Him as our Lord and Savior, Jesus Christ. He sent His Spirit to be our comforter and our guide, and all of His strength is always available to us. It is ironic, but many people have come to a closer relationship with Christ as a result of attending AA meetings. I believe this happens because alcoholics, or those who love them, are incapable of restoring their lives to sanity on their own. They realize the necessity of relying on God. God is able to transform lives and instill love and purpose in lives that were miserable and aimless. This is why a "recovering alcoholic" is often a person who is vibrantly alive and may actually thank God for the valleys that he or she had to walk through. I wish I had the freedom to share God's love with my class.

I'll always wonder about Becky and about the student so concerned about her friend. I get excited when I hear success stories like the one Doug shared, "My father is an entirely different guy now that he doesn't drink anymore. There is a twinkle in his eye again."

If alcohol is causing problems in your life seek help immediately. There are many resources available to you. Go to a pastor, a teacher, a counselor—any adult whom you trust. Make sure the eyes you look out of or look into always retain their twinkle.

1ST Place

When You Don't  Up

I Have a Friend Who Makes Herself Vomit. What Do I Do?

I wasn't at all surprised when Sue took first place. She took first almost every weekend. It was getting to be a habit with her. The manager of the speech contest called her category. She sat with clenched fists as he announced third and second places. When her name wasn't called, she gripped the sides of her chair, closed her eyes, and held her breath. And then he called her name. Sue was out of her seat in a flash and rushed forward to receive her trophy—one more for her collection.

As Sue came back to her seat, the other students on the speech team hugged her. I added my congratulations. I was happy for Sue, but at the same time I was concerned—winning had become such an obsession with her. One week when she hadn't taken first place, she became almost suicidal. As her coach, I had come to realize that she needed constant approval. Sue was the only student on the team who came to my room after school each evening to practice her recitation. Most students came in once or twice a week. She regarded any criticism—from me or a judge—as a personal attack. Criticism devastated her. She was addicted to approval and perfection— an addiction I deal with myself.

Sue sat right behind me on the bus on the way home to Brainerd, her trophy still clenched in her right hand. When we stopped to eat, she and the girl she was sitting with were the first off the bus. The other speech team members poured into the restaurant, and I could hear one of the workers shout to his fellow employees, "We've a bus coming in!" Stacks of burgers were suddenly thrown onto the grill and bags of fries into the deep-fat fryer.

I ordered a chef salad with french and blue cheese dressing and a diet cola. I turned to find a place to sit when Sue and her friend Michele said, "Come sit with us, Mr. Doud."

"Thank you. I will." I sat across from Sue, noticing she had brought the trophy into the restaurant with her. It sat across from me, a female figurine decked out with a laurel wreath. "How many trophies do you have now, Sue?" I asked.

"Thirteen," she said, "but not all of them are first place trophies."

Michelle exclaimed, "Wow! I'd be happy to receive just one."

Sue beamed and took a sip of her drink.

"Aren't you eating, Sue?" I asked.

"I'm not very hungry," she said, "but I will eat one of your french fries, Michelle."

"Sure," Michelle answered, "help yourself. Eat all you want."

Sue took a french fry and ate it. She took a couple of sips from her diet cola and then asked us to excuse her for a minute because she had to go to the bathroom. As Sue went into the bathroom, Michelle turned to me and said, "She's going to the bathroom to make herself vomit up that french fry."

"What?" I asked. I couldn't believe it.

"Sue is anorexic, didn't you know that?"

"No." I was shocked. "One french fry?"

"She thinks she's fat. She went to treatment last summer and was better for a while after she came home, but now she hardly eats at all. And when she does, she usually makes herself vomit it up."

"How in the world can she think she is fat? I could practically put both my hands around her waist." I was dumbfounded.

"She does think she's fat. Oh, here she comes." Michelle and I grew quickly quiet.

When Sue was seated, I didn't know what to say. She detected my uneasiness. "Is something wrong?" she asked.

I was at a loss for words—something that rarely happens to me. I wish I could report that I was led to confront Sue and talk with her about her eating disorder, but I was totally caught off guard. After making some comment about how we had to get going, I found myself rounding up the rest of my speech students and leading them back to the bus. I did vow to talk with Sue's counselor and find out more about her problem.

I wasn't unfamiliar with anorexia or with bulimia. When I went from 327 pounds to 165 pounds in one year, I had forced myself to regurgitate with some regularity. It became a habit that was very hard to break. I loved to eat, but I would feel guilty whenever I had eaten more than I thought I should have. Along with the guilt I also experienced fear. I was frightened that I would wake up the following morning and be fat again. The combination of guilt and fear often proved overwhelming, and I would force myself to vomit. At first I found it difficult to make myself regurgitate, but eventually it became quite easy. When I developed this habit I had never heard of any eating disorder other than obesity. The words *bulimia* and *anorexia nervosa* were not yet in my vocabulary.

A number of years ago something happened to open everyone's eyes to the devastating results of continued purging. A well-known singer, Karen Carpenter, half of the brother-sister combo called "The Carpenters," died as a result of anorexia. Suddenly it was the topic of news programs and television talk shows. Workshops were held for school teachers and other helping professionals. We learned that as many as 30 percent of adolescent girls have some type of eating disorder.

I always wondered about the boys. Didn't they experience eating disorders too? I have since discovered what I already knew to be true: Boys can become anorexic or bulimic too. It just doesn't happen with the same frequency as it does with girls.

Some people confuse bulimia and anorexia. Anorexia nervosa is an illness characterized by a preoccupation with being thin. Anorexics have a fear of gaining weight and will develop all types of behaviors in an attempt to lose weight. Bulimia is characterized by binge eating followed by self-induced vomiting. Bulimics will often eat great quantities of food and then force themselves to regurgitate.

Fortunately, I never developed the habit of eating and purging and eating and purging, nor did I become obsessed with being thin. I was able to stop the practice of vomiting willfully once I realized how dangerous it was. Most people who make purging a practice actually become addicted to it. They can stop doing it no easier than an alcoholic can stop drinking. Therapy and treatment are usually needed to break an eating disorder.

Several years ago I read a story in the *Minneapolis Star and Tribune* that still haunts me. It was the story of a 17-year-old girl from a small town in Minnesota. According to the article, the girl's boyfriend had told her that her "butt was too big." She became so conscious of her size that she stopped eating. Whenever she did eat, which was seldom, she forced herself to purge afterwards. Her weight fell dramatically. Her parents and her friends and her teachers became concerned. Her weight plunged to 81 pounds. Finally, she was confronted and she agreed to enter a treatment center. After being discharged from the treatment center, she eventually went back to her practice of forced purging. Emotionally, she was on a roller coaster. She hated herself and believed herself to be fat. She was a straight A student and a homecoming queen—a girl who had established impossibly high expectations. When she couldn't meet all of her expectations, life seemed totally unmanageable. She was miserable. One day, after recording a message for her family on a tape recorder, she drove to a nearby state park, poured two gallons of gasoline over herself, and set herself on fire.

What was she feeling when she lit the match? How much pain did she experience as she burned to death? How did her parents react when they were notified? These questions have haunted me for years.

If you or someone you know has an eating disorder, please seek professional help immediately. Seek out a school counselor, your doctor, your pastor, or a trusted adult friend. Bulimia and anorexia are serious diseases. Some people incorrectly believe that only a very few people with bulimia or anorexia develop serious medical complications. The truth is that eating disorders wreak havoc on the body.

One of the most recognizable characteristics of both bulimia and anorexia is erosion of the teeth. Think of it. Stomach acids are strong enough to digest food. People who force themselves to purge also force up stomach acids that will corrode the teeth. Untreated eating disorders lead to impaired brain function. Bulimic and anorexic patients often develop chronic depression and become suicidal.

Anorexics like Karen Carpenter literally starve themselves to death. When someone starves, the heart becomes weak. A weakened heart affects the entire body: blood pressure falls; kidneys quit functioning; new blood cells aren't produced; and anemia, fatigue, and weakness result. Ironically, metabolism is reduced, and in females, the menstrual period often stops.

After my experience with Sue and after the death of Karen Carpenter, I read and studied a lot about eating disorders. A few years later one of my students told me she had used ipecac, a syrup used to induce vomiting in cases of accidental poisoning. She was fortunate to be alive. Anorexics who use ipecac to induce vomiting risk permanent damage to the heart. Bulimics who use ipecac may die of cardiac arrest. True, adverse symptoms do not develop overnight. Most eating disorders are developed in adolescence and secretly practiced into adulthood. Eventually the disorder will begin to manifest itself with all of its tremendously damaging characteristics. It is essential to treat the illness before irreparable harm has been done to the body.

Most victims of eating disorders approach life as Sue did. Can you see her clutching on to her trophy? Studies reveal that the typical anorexic or bulimic is a perfectionist who has set extremely high expectations for herself or himself. She or he often suffers from low self-esteem and depression.

I mentioned earlier that I had more than a tendency toward perfectionism. Growing up, I always desperately sought everyone's approval. I had the feeling that I would not receive the approval I sought unless I was perfect. In order to be loved, I had to be perfect. I even saw God as someone who would love me more if I could only do more to please Him. If only I would go to church more, memorize more Scripture verses, give more money to the church, eliminate all my bad habits, etc. etc.—then He would love me more. I realize now that I had bought into one of Satan's most crafty lies. I believed that my self-worth was directly related to my performance. When you buy this type of lie, you believe that God's love is conditional. That type of love is very common in the world today. It is the type of love that says, "I will love you as long as . . ." What was hard for me to learn and what is hard for many people to learn is that God does not put any conditions on His love. God's love is unconditional.

The Bible is filled with story after story of God's love for people in spite of their failures. Jesus is perfect. But to accomplish His will, God used not only His perfect Son, but also imperfect Noah and Abraham; Rahab, the prostitute; the persecutor of Christians—Paul; and hot-headed, stubborn Peter.

The Bible tells us clearly that we—and Noah and Rahab and all the rest—are saved by God's grace. Like the familiar saying says, "If we had been perfect or could have become perfect, we wouldn't have needed a Savior."

If you tend to be a perfectionist, too, please take note. Trust in God's unconditional love and quit trying to earn love by measuring up. You are a valuable person—important enough for Jesus to die for. Share this message with a friend who needs to hear it.

Remember: If you or someone you know is the victim of an eating disorder, get help immediately. It is worth the risk of losing a friend to save a friend.

Save the First Dance for Me

*Am I the Only One Who
Isn't Sexually Active?*

I took their tickets and said, "Have a good time." Like most of the couples coming to the dance, they were eager to get into the gym and they didn't answer me. I grabbed the tickets from the next couple in line. "Hope you enjoy the dance," I said. At least they nodded as they almost ran into the gym where a live band was playing its version of some top-20 hit.

I had been taking tickets for only about 20 minutes, and a large number of my fellow high school students were already out on the dance floor. From the ticket counter I could see fellow Staples' Cardinals shaking their bodies and putting themselves through all kinds of strange contortions. Some of them looked as though they were in pain.

"Yo! Gus! Here are our tickets, man!" I turned to see Joe and Rachel and three other

couples standing in line, waiting to enter the dance. Where had they all come from?

"Sorry," I said as I took their tickets. They quickly headed toward the dance floor where the band was beginning its first slow song of the evening.

I watched as the couples held one another close. One tall basketball player looked funny bending over his short girlfriend. He was almost bent in half as he kissed her neck. That's disgusting, I thought jealously.

Gus. Joe had called me Gus. I hated being called Gus. It was a name I had picked up when I was a sophomore, and I didn't have anyone to blame for it except myself. One of our assignments in speech class was to explain our nicknames. I listened as some of my peers shared their nicknames. Joe was "Studman." Steve was "Moose." Larry was "The Professor." Scott was "Ironman." Rachel was "Baby Doll." I never had a nickname. I thought maybe I should call myself "Hippoman" since I regarded myself as not only the fattest, but also the ugli-est, kid in our class. Mom was always telling me how good-looking she thought I was. Huh. If I were good-looking, I'd be out there on the dance floor right now. My thoughts went back to speech class.

"And what is your nickname, Guy?" the speech teacher had asked.

"I don't have one," I answered.

"I want everyone to come up with one for the class," he said, "so figure one out for yourself, okay?"

When he asked me later what I had chosen for a nickname, I said "Gus." Don't ask me why. I may have simply chosen it as an alternative to "Guy." I was often teased about my name. "Why didn't your parents just call you 'boy'?" I heard that wise remark often. "If you had been a female, would your parents have named you 'girl'?" was another. I pretended to take the joking in stride, but it hurt down deep inside.

My thoughts came back to the present, and I stood staring at Studman and Baby Doll, practically making out on the dance floor. I said to myself, "Gus is really a stupid nickname."

"You can go dance now, Guy, if you like." I turned and saw Mr. Rengel, the assistant principal.

"That's okay," I said. "I don't mind taking tickets."

"How come you don't have a date tonight?" Mr. Rengel asked.

"I was going to come with Ali McGraw, but then she died," I joked.

Mr. Rengel laughed politely, but I don't think he understood my attempt at humor. Ali McGraw, a beautiful young movie actress, had recently appeared in a movie called *Love Story* opposite Ryan O'Neal. I had gone to see the movie eight times. Every time, I flooded the floor around my seat with tears as cancer killed Ali, while Ryan, whose nickname was "Preppy" in the movie, faithfully remained by her side. I looked at Mr. Rengel, your stereotypical assistant principal, and I doubted that he had even seen *Love Story* or knew who Ali McGraw was.

That's the way it often was when I was a teenager. I wondered if any adult could understand how I felt. Was there anyone who could possibly understand how I felt this night as I looked out at my classmates locked together on the dance floor? Was I the only student in Staples High School who didn't have a girlfriend?

Joe and Rachel said, "Good night, Gus," as they walked by me, heading for the exit. Were they leaving the dance already? Was the band that bad? I thought they sounded pretty good.

Mr. Rengel stopped them. "If you leave you can't get back in," he said.

"We know," said Studman as he and Rachel headed out the door.

"I wonder what they are going to do?" Mr. Rengel asked, although I don't think he really expected me to answer.

I had heard of a few keg parties planned for the evening, and I wondered if that was where Joe was taking Baby Doll. I had never been to a keg party, and some of my classmates had been on my case to go. "You're a senior, Gus! Loosen up, man!" I heard the words ringing in my ear, "Loosen up, man!" "Loosen up, man!" "Loosen up, man!"

I thought back to the conversation I had heard on the football team bus several weeks earlier. I was the manager of the football team. That meant that I was in charge of the equipment. I also got to run out on the field during time-outs and make sure that our players got a drink of water. Although Mr. Rengel, who was also the athletic director, awarded me a letter, I didn't really feel I was part of the team. In my dreams, I always wanted to be the quarterback.

We were on our way home from an away game in Aitkin, about 60 miles from Staples. It was a Friday night, and some of the guys toward the back of the bus were talking about what they were going to do when they got back to town. As they compared notes, several mentioned that their girlfriends would be waiting for them. I was sitting right ahead of Joe, the Studman, and Ironman Scott. I couldn't help overhearing their conversation.

"Whatcha got goin' tonight?" Scott asked.

"Gonna meet up with Rachel," Joe answered.

"You guys are pretty serious, aren't you?" Scott asked.

"Yeah," was Joe's answer.

"Is she giving you any?" Scott asked.

"Man, oh man," Joe said, "she is one hot chick! What about you and Becky?"

"She made me promise not to tell anyone," Scott said, laughing.

"You didn't say a word," Joe laughed.

My face burned. I wanted to crawl under the seat. You may find this hard to believe, but I was so naive that I didn't think that kind of thing happened in Staples. Joe and Scott continued to share the details of their sex lives, joking about their girlfriends and the size of their breasts and commenting on what a hassle it was when one of their girlfriends had to refrain from intercourse because she was having her period. My face burned hotter and hotter.

Bill, who was sitting next to me—I don't know if he had a nickname or not—turned around and joined Joe and Scott in their discussion. I don't remember who Bill was going out with, but it seems that he had "scored" too.

"What about you, Gus? I suppose you're still a virgin?" Joe asked the question.

I didn't answer. My cheeks were ablaze. Was being a Christian worth it? Why couldn't I be normal like everyone else? I took out a tissue to blow my nose. Why does your nose always run when you start to cry? Thankfully my tears were unseen in the darkness of the school bus that black October night.

In 1975 I began my teaching career at Brainerd Senior High School in Brainerd, Minnesota. Although I was still naive about some things, I had learned quite a bit about "the real world" during my four years of college. I had found good fellowship with other Christians and had learned that, even though many of my classmates were sexually active, there was a group of us who took our commitment to Christ seriously and wanted to save our first sexual experience for the person we would someday marry. Given my track record when it came to dating, I doubted that I'd ever be married. I feared I was going to be a virgin my entire life.

Survey results conducted among Minnesota high school students my first few years of teaching indicated what I knew to be true: A large percentage of junior and senior high school students are sexually active. It seems as though having sex at an early age is now viewed as one of those things "everyone does" when they're a kid. But from my work with teenagers I can factually state, "No, everyone doesn't do it." In fact, more and more Christian young people are taking bold stands and actually signing pledges, promising that they will be true to God's design for their lives and keep themselves sexually pure for the one God will lead them to marry.

One night after I had spoken to a group of teenagers, I offered to stay and talk to individuals. Vicki was the first to seek me out. A very attractive girl, Vicki was a cheerleader and involved in numerous school activities. "I love Jesus," she said.

"I can see His love in your eyes," I said, "but I can also see that you are troubled by something. What is it?"

"What you were talking about . . . I want to do it," Vicki said, but she seemed apprehensive. I knew she meant that she wanted to keep herself sexually pure.

I had talked very frankly with this group about sex and had told them to "save the first dance" for the person God would someday lead them to marry. "Save the first dance" was my way of saying "save yourself." I had explained how intercourse is God's special gift for married people. When two people come together as one during the act of intercourse, it is more than just a physical experience. Two hearts become one. In marriage, joys are doubled and sorrows are shared. I believe the physical act of love-making between married people confirms the spiritual union that the couple shares in Jesus Christ. Any sexual act performed outside of marriage cheapens the loving experience God intended intercourse to be.

"I want to save the first dance for the man I marry," Vicki said.

"Good for you," I said.

"But it's not easy, Mr. Doud. I've been going with this guy for three years now. Prom is coming up in about a month. My boyfriend said that most of his friends are getting motel rooms for the night, and he told me that if I didn't want to do it, he was going to ask somebody else to prom."

"I suppose you look at your friends, and you know that many of them are sexually active. You wonder why you should be the only virgin, right?"

"Well, even some of my best Christian friends say times have changed and that as long as you practice safe sex, it's okay. Some of them have told me that I don't know what I'm missing."

"Do you believe that?" I asked.

"No. My pastor always says that times may change, but God's Word doesn't."

"Hey, your pastor is right on."

"What do I do about my boyfriend? We've been going together for three years and I really love him a lot."

"I don't think he has much love for you, Vicki," I said.

"How can you say that? You don't even know him. He's a Christian too." She seemed almost angry.

"True love shows respect. Your boyfriend doesn't respect your decision to want to keep yourself sexually pure. I'm going to tell you the truth: He is more concerned about what he deems to be his own sexual needs than he is about your making a decision that could change your whole life. If he really loves you, he'll think even more of you for standing up for what you know God wants you to do."

"That's what my pastor said," Vicki said with a smile.

"Your pastor is a smart man," I said, and laughed. "You say that your boyfriend is a Christian?"

"Yeah, he's even the head of the youth group at his church."

"Do you two ever pray together?"

Vicki gave me a look that seemed to say, "Join the 20th century, Mr. Doud."

"What would happen," I asked, "if you asked your boyfriend to pray with you about where your relationship is at and where God wants it to go?" Vicki could see that I was dead serious.

"He'd think I was crazy."

"Then I think you'd better find another boyfriend."

"But we've been going together for three years. I really want to go to prom. I have my dress already picked out. If I don't go with Tom, no one will ask me because they'll all still think I'm going with him."

"I know that the prom is a big event for you right now. A few years from now, though, when you get to be my age, it will be just another memory. Hopefully, it will be a good memory, not a memory where you look back and realize that you made a decision that you'll forever regret."

Vicki just stared at me as though she thought that if she could convince me why she should go to the prom with Tom, it would be okay.

"Vicki, I have a question for you. You mentioned that many of your girlfriends are having sex with their boyfriends. How many of them do you think will be married to the boyfriend they are going out with now?"

"I doubt that any of them will even stay together after high school."

"I doubt it too. So they've established a bad precedent, don't you think?"

"What do you mean?" Vicki asked.

"There's a country-western song that jokes about loving the one you're with. That's what I see happening with teenagers and adults who are dating. Movies, television, popular novels, and secular music all glamorize having sex with whomever you feel attracted to. By the time many people reach the age of 25, they have had a multitude of sexual partners. Sex is no longer a loving gift, it is merely a physical act. For many people who reach this stage, sex never becomes what God intended it to be. They have developed a habit of seeing sex as something you to do to relieve sexual pressure. They may get married, but then they may start to lose interest in their spouse because, after a while, sex becomes rather routine. You see, for many people who were sexually active before marriage, sex after marriage doesn't have the same excitement. It becomes routine. So, guess what?"

"They start looking for other sexual partners?" Vicki had been listening intently to my sermonette.

"Bingo! Then often one divorce follows another, and that cycle is passed down to the children. Studies show that a husband and wife who are both virgins when they get married are much more likely to stay married for a lifetime than a couple where one or both partners have been sexually active." I paused for a moment. "Vicki, there is so much more at stake than you can even begin to realize."

"I have just one more question, Mr. Doud," Vicki said. "If you make a mistake and commit a sin, doesn't God forgive you?"

"You bet He does, Vicki. When we ask for God's forgiveness, not only does He forgive our sin, the Bible says that He no longer remembers it. He removes our sin from us as far as the east is from the west."

I thought I could tell what Vicki was thinking: even though God forgives us for our sin, there are still consequences. "I know a man who has AIDS, Vicki. He is now a dynamic Christian. God has forgiven him for his behavior that led to his contacting AIDS. He is forgiven, Vicki, but he still has AIDS."

As I prayed with Vicki that night, I wasn't sure what decision she would eventually make. She is just one of millions of teenagers who are at a mighty big crossroads in their lives. There is a tremendous amount of pressure to give in. Some succumb to the pressure of their boyfriend or girlfriend or to that of their peers. Some decide to have sex as an act of rebellion against authority. Some are desperately seeking love and mistakenly believe that if they "give themselves" to someone else, that person will forever be indebted and will always be there for them. I have seen many teenagers who couldn't believe it when their boyfriend dumped them for someone else. More than once I've heard these words spoken through tears, "He used me, and then he dumped me."

Some teenagers are sexually active because it has already become a habit. Some become sexually active because everything they have seen in the movies and on television suggests that it is the thing to do. And some teenagers, with God's help, commit themselves to sexual abstinence.

I realized on the plane as I was flying back to Minnesota that I hadn't even talked to Vicki about the risk of sexually transmitted diseases. My experience is that most teenagers believe that the person with whom they choose to have sex couldn't possibly be infected. They hear statistics like this one, "According to the United States Department of Health and Human Services and the Centers for Disease Control, sexually transmitted diseases infect three million teenagers annually." For some strange reason they don't think they have the possibility of being one of those three million. This mistaken attitude is the soil that will keep AIDS and syphilis and gonorrhea growing and spreading like quack grass in a fertile field.

I realize, too, how hard it is for kids like Vicki to abstain from sex. Not only are they bombarded with sex by music and by the media, but even our government and our schools send them mixed messages. We tell them to say no to drugs, but yes to safe sex. No one will argue with the fact that there really isn't any safe sex, and yet the Centers for Disease Control and the city of New York recently distributed a brochure entitled "Teens Have the Right." The brochure contains six statements called a "Teenager's Bill of Rights."

- I have the right to think for myself.
- I have the right to decide whether to have sex and whom to have it with.
- I have the right to use protection when I have sex.
- I have the right to buy and use condoms.
- I have the right to express myself.
- I have the right to ask for help if I need it.

I wonder what Vicki would think if she read that "Bill of Rights." If you are being bombarded with this type of propaganda, I would encourage you to remember what God has to say about all of this. God states that adultery is sin. He created your sexuality as a good gift and wants you to know the joy of "becoming one" with your husband or wife. The only truly safe sex is sex between a husband and wife who have had and have no other sexual partners. Express yourself? God has given you many wonderful gifts. Use them to bring glory to His kingdom. If you are tempted to abuse your gift of sexuality, ask for help, seek out the wisdom of spiritual mentors—committed believers who can show you God's will and help lead you in the way that's pleasing to Him.

What about those kids who have already been sexually active? Unfortunately, they have missed out on what God had intended to be one of the greatest moments of their lives—that moment on their wedding night when, for the first time, a man gives himself to his wife and the wife gives herself to her husband, and they become one flesh, united in hopes and aims and love. There is only one first time. However, if a person who has been or is sexually active outside of marriage is moved to repent, God does forgive. God's forgiveness in Jesus washes us clean and gives us a fresh start.

I realize that the road I walk is pretty narrow. Many do consider me old fashioned. I don't care. I can look down the highway a few years and see your husband or your wife standing beside you. I can hear his or her question, "Did you save the first dance for me?"

George Washington Comes to Staples

Why Is There So Much Racial Prejudice and Hatred?

I grew up in Staples, Minnesota, a small town almost smack dab in the middle of the "Land of Ten Thousand Lakes." (Actually, there are more than ten thousand! I counted!)

Staples was a great place to grow up. In the neighborhood where I lived, neighbors knocked on your door and asked if they could borrow a couple of eggs. Sometimes they would drop off a dozen cookies, if they had just made a batch. People shared. People cared. There was a true sense of community.

My dad worked for the Staples Police Department. For most of his years on the force there was only the chief, my dad, and two other officers. My mom carried a badge, too, but the only times she was called into service were when a female got intoxicated and needed to be

thrown in the local jail that served as the town's "drunk tank."

I only remember my mom responding to a call once or twice. I remember her coming home late one night after she had helped arrest a very intoxicated lady. The lady had taken a swing at my mom, and from what I hear, mom took her billy club and gave the lady a swat on the side of the head. The lady threatened a law suit against my mom and the city of Staples, but nothing ever came of it. I don't think the woman even knew why she had a bump on her head when she woke the next morning.

Most of my dad's work as a policeman was rather routine, too, although once he did help capture and arrest some convicts who had escaped from prison. I tell that story in my book *Molder of Dreams.* You should read it! The governor of Minnesota honored my father for his bravery. I was proud of my dad. Most of the time, however, Dad spent his time as a Staples police officer issuing speeding tickets and making sure that people who shouldn't be driving didn't. I don't ever remember him investigating any burglaries or robberies, although I'm sure there must have been a few in Staples. I probably just never heard about them, because, you see, Staples people just didn't believe in crime.

That's why I found it so hard to understand why, in other parts of the United States, people were rioting and killing one another. I didn't believe it when I saw pictures that showed that, in some parts of our country, black people and white people were not allowed to drink out of the same drinking fountain. When we finally got a television, I saw news reports of fighting in the streets in Los Angeles, and I heard clips of speeches by Martin Luther King. I couldn't understand why people couldn't get along. I guess I was a young idealist, but I knew that America had been founded on the principle that all people are created equal.

Now, I must admit that I never knew any people of a different color from my own when I was growing up. There just weren't any in Staples at the time. There was an Indian reservation about 50 miles away, but I don't even remember any Native Americans coming to town. No, Staples was mostly a blend of people of German, Polish, Irish, and Scandinavian heritage. Each year Faith Lutheran Church would hold its annual lutefisk supper, and one of the German Catholic churches out in the country would sponsor its yearly sauerkraut-and-brats feed. Leftsa and krumkakka were regular treats, and everyone seemed to enjoy the best of everyone else's heritage. The Andersons, the Johnsons, the Larsons, and the Petersons would sit down in church fellowship halls with the Murphys, the Martins, the Wilkowskis, and the O'Reillys. And "a good time would be enjoyed by all."

I wish I could say that Staples was free of prejudice, but it wasn't. I heard people talk about what was going on in other parts of our country. I remember hearing things like, "We should send all the niggers back to Africa." I knew that the term *nigger* was offensive to Americans of African descent, and it hurt me when adults I looked up to spoke in this fashion. I truly didn't understand why people couldn't get along. Maybe as a result of these spoken prejudices, I grew up believing certain stereotypes too. Was everything that had a made-in-Japan sticker really junk? Were all Native Americans really "drunkards"? Were Polish people as dumb as all the jokes suggested? Why did all the jokes about Irishmen start this way, "Two Irishmen were sitting in a bar . . ."?

Not only did I learn about racial prejudice and hatred, I discovered that some people are uncomfortable with others whose religious or political views are different from their own. I learned this in a most dramatic way.

In 1960 John Kennedy ran for president against Richard Nixon. Kennedy was a Catholic and a Democrat. Nixon was a Quaker and a Republican. I was only seven years old at the time, but I remember what happened as though it were yesterday.

I grew up in a strong Democratic family. Wait a minute now, don't stereotype me! The truth is that most young children adopt the political and religious beliefs of their parents. My parents were staunch Democrats. I grew up being taught that Democrats were for the poor, blue-collar, working people and that Republicans were for the white-collar business types who had a lot of money. So, it is only logical that my parents strongly supported John Fitzgerald Kennedy. My dad talked with a passion about how Kennedy just had to get elected to help "the little guy." I remember lying awake at night fearing what would happen if Nixon did get elected and I even prayed to God, asking Him to "make all the voters vote for Kennedy."

Our little house on the south side of Staples—the south side wasn't as prestigious as the north side—proudly displayed a "Kennedy for President" sign in the front yard. Everyone in our family wore "Kennedy for President" buttons. This was America, and you had a right to support whomever you wanted for president, right? Well, something happened one day that will forever stay etched in my mind.

Since the Staples police force was so small, it only had one car. Whenever an officer finished his shift he would drive to the home of the officer relieving him. My dad always sat in his chair reading, his gun and holster on, his hat and coat hanging behind the front door, waiting to go to work. My job was to watch for the police car. When the Staples cruiser pulled up in front, I'd say, "Dad, it's time to go to work." He'd say, "Thanks, boy," and he'd get out of his chair, grab his hat and coat, say good-bye to mom and me, and go out to begin his shift.

That was the usual routine, but one day the police car pulled up in front of the house on one of Dad's days off. I saw it pull up and I asked, "Dad, are you supposed to be ready to go to work?"

"No," he answered, "it's my day off." He stood and looked at the policeman coming up the walk. Dad went to the front door and his fellow officer came into the house. They exchanged small talk, Dad reassuring himself that it was his day off. Then Dad asked, "What's up?"

"Well, Jess," the other officer said, "it's about that Kennedy sign in your front yard. Since you are a city employee, I think you should take it down."

Dad just stared at his fellow officer for a moment before he answered, "I have just as much right to have a sign in my yard as anyone else."

"But, Jess," the other officer continued hesitantly, "Kennedy is a Catholic."

I believe Dad swore and asked what that had to do with anything.

I'll never forget the other officer's answer: "If Kennedy is elected, he'll turn the country over to the pope."

I don't remember the rest of the conversation, probably because my young mind was trying to understand how the pope could rule our country. I was a Protestant. I didn't know much about the pope, except that I had heard that Catholics believed he took his orders directly from God and so they took their orders directly from him. All I do remember is that the Kennedy sign stayed up in our yard. Kennedy won by a very slim margin, and as far as I know, he never took his orders from the pope. Years later I would learn that Kennedy was the first Catholic president ever elected and that many people throughout America—not just in Staples—had been afraid of having a Catholic in the White House.

Today we would regard such a fear as ridiculous, wouldn't we? We know better, don't we? You see, the source of much of our racial, political, and religious prejudice is ignorance and fear: We simply don't know any better.

I'll never forget the first time I met a "person of color."

Like most kids in Staples, I was introduced to people of color through magazines, the newspaper, and television. I remember asking my grandfather once how come there weren't any black people living in Staples. "It's too cold for them here," he said, and I took his answer as a logical explanation. In fact, the entire state of Minnesota, where I live, has a very small percentage of people whom we classify as minorities in our country. I assumed that people who came from Mexico or Africa probably couldn't handle Minnesota winters and so they avoided our land of frozen lakes. (Even a lot of Minnesotans find it necessary to hightail it out of here come November!)

For as long as I can remember, Staples has been a hub for the railroad. It is only one of a few cities in all of Minnesota where you can still catch a passenger train. You can get on the train in Staples and ride almost anywhere. The railroad of my youth, the railroad that my grandfather served for many years, was the Northern Pacific, which Grandpa called the NP. The NP is no more. The Burlington Northern Railroad now runs passenger trains out of Staples. As a kid, I used to love to go to the depot and watch the trains—especially the passenger trains—come in. The smells and the sounds still seem very real to me. I close my eyes and hear the click of the huge steel wheels as they meet new track. I sense a familiar mixture of steam and diesel fuel and groaning as the giant metal snake lumbers to a stop.

When I was in second grade, we rode the passenger train from Staples to Wadena, 18 miles away. In Wadena we had a picnic in the city park and then we rode the train back to Staples. I'll never forget it. I dreamed of how exciting it would be to ride the train through the mountains all the way to Seattle. But I had to settle for Wadena.

One day, when I was still very young, I watched a passenger train pull in to the Staples depot. I saw the conductor step down from the doorway and put the customary stool at the bottom of the stairs leading from the train. He was dressed like all the other conductors I had seen. He wore a sharp, black hat and suit. But not only was the suit black, so was he. He was the first black man I had ever seen.

I realized that I was staring at him, but I knew he couldn't see me. He smiled as he said good-bye to each of the passengers and helped them off the train. After helping all the passengers off the train, he headed for the depot where I stood at the window, still watching him. He was only a few feet from me as he came through the door and walked up to the ticket window to ask the train master a question. He was as black as the night. I wondered if his skin felt the same as a white person's. He must have felt my eyes burning holes into his head because he turned around and stared right at me. He smiled. "Hi, son," he said, "how you doing?'"

I tried to answer him, but the words didn't come. The next thing I knew I was out of the depot and on my bike on my way home. Why was I so frightened? I felt ashamed that I had acted in such a ridiculous manner.

I acted much more sensibly the day that George Washington came to Staples. I wasn't at the depot when the passenger train pulled into town. I suspect it arrived in much the same the way it did every other day. My dad was on duty when the train arrived, so he was the police officer who received the rather peculiar call from the depot. It seemed that there was a passenger aboard the train who was asking for assistance. My dad went to the depot, met the passenger, listened to his request, and—with the true spirit of a Staples police officer—was more than happy to oblige.

I don't remember what I was doing when Dad pulled up in front our house in the squad car, but I'll never forget what happened afterwards. Dad got out of the car and started walking up the front sidewalk toward our house. I ran to meet him. "Come on," he said, "there's someone I want you meet." He turned and started back to the car.

I could see two people sitting in the back seat of the police car. One was big and one was small. They both were black.

I didn't even have time to think about how I should act. The next thing you know, Dad was opening the front seat of the car and introducing me to the folks in the back. I don't remember what the adult said his name was, but he asked me mine. "I'm Guy Doud," I said.

The adult answered, "Hi, Guy, this is my son."

The son appeared to be about my age. He smiled at me and said, "Hi, I'm George Washington."

George Washington? I think I said something like "I've never met a president before."

Both the father and his son laughed.

"Mr. Washington and his son are from Chicago," Dad said. "They just got into town on the train."

I remembered the conductor I had run from and wondered if he had been their conductor too.

Dad continued, "They have several hours before the train leaves again, and since George has never been out of Chicago before, Mr. Washington was wondering if someone could take him out in the country and show him a farm and some farm animals. I thought maybe you'd like to come along."

I rode with my dad and George Washington and his dad out to a farm not far from Dower Lake, about three miles out of town. The farmer showed us around his farm as though George really were the president. I have to admit, I didn't know much more about farms than George did, and I had never milked a cow either. The farmer asked George if he would like to try milking a cow, and when he finished I asked if I could too. George was a lot better at milking than I was. I was frightened I was going to hurt the cow's teat.

On the way back to the depot, George Washington and I compared notes about what it was like growing up in the inner city of Chicago and in rural Staples, Minnesota. Despite the facts that our skin was a different color and we lived in different places, I remember thinking, George is just like me. He was a big baseball fan, too, although he didn't like the Minnesota Twins. He liked the Chicago Cubs.

We got back to the depot just a few minutes before it was time for George Washington and his father to reboard the North Coast Limited. George walked over to the water fountain and had a drink. When he shook my hand good-bye, I couldn't understand why anyone would think that George and I shouldn't drink out of the same water fountain.

I've often wondered about George Washington since. I've never forgotten my trip to the farm with him and his dad. I've never milked a cow since. I wonder if George has. I have four children. I wonder if George is married and has any kids. My dad died in 1985. I wonder if Mr. Washington is still alive. When the Minnesota Twins won the World Series in 1987 and in 1991, do you think George thought of me?

As a child of the '60s, I was glad when I heard that Rosa Parks refused to give up her seat on a bus. I sang along with the marchers as I watched them on television singing "We Shall Overcome." When I heard Martin Luther King speak so eloquently about his dream, I knew that it was a dream that I shared. As I learned more and more about what it means to be a Christian, I realized more and more that there is one God and we are all His children. There is no place for racial prejudice or hatred in God's kingdom.

In more recent years I've rejoiced with the Asian boat people and those from third-world countries to whom the United States has opened its doors. I remember that the Germans and the Polish and the Irish and the Scandinavians were once refugees too. Lady Liberty Enlightening the World welcomed them all.

I know that many feel that America can no longer reach out to the rest of the world. I've heard people say, "We must take care of our own." I believe that the source of much racial prejudice stems from this belief that there isn't "enough to go around" and "we must first take care of ourselves." Many Americans are afraid that these people who seem different will take away their jobs and destroy the standard of living to which they have become accustomed.

Some people seem to believe that those who have a religion other than Christianity stand to destroy the Christian base of our nation. So in the name of Christ, they condone racial prejudice and hatred. This is ironic when you consider that it was Christ who said that we are to love our neighbors as ourselves and share His love with people from all nations. It was Christ who said, "I tell you the truth, whatever you did not do for one of the least of these [brothers of mine], you did not do for Me" (Matthew 25:45).

I believe that God will teach us how to share. He can meet all of the physical needs of all people, just as He did when Jesus fed the 5,000. Continuing to harbor racial prejudice is not compatible with Christian faith.

I'll never forget watching George Washington board the train. I waved to him and to the conductor who had just called, "All aboard!"

A Conversation in and about the Heavens

How Do I Share My Faith without Sounding like a Nerd?

"Are you sure there arc no seats where I don't have to have someone sitting next to me? I get claustrophobic."

"I'm sorry, sir, but I'm showing all seats filled."

I walked away from the airline ticket counter reminding myself how much I hated to fly. It wasn't so bad if I could get a seat where no one was sitting next to me, but if I ended up sandwiched between two other people in a three-seat row I resolved never to fly again. There were other reasons besides physical discomfort for my not wanting to sit next to anyone. Despite the fact that I am a well-known speaker, I actually am quite a shy person. Invariably someone always asks me, "And what do you do for a living?"

Now when asked this question, I realize I do have several options, but each option has its pluses and minuses. I can say, "I'm a teacher," but then they want to know why I'm not teaching. I can say, "I am a motivational speaker," but then they always want to know what I speak about. (One time a guy insisted I give him part of my speech as we were flying over the Grand Canyon on the way to Phoenix.) The truth is that most of the time when I speak, I talk about Jesus. And when I'm not speaking for the Lord, I'm actively involved in the ministry of my church. The first time I shared this fact with someone, she grabbed her cocktail and said, "Oh, you look smarter than that!"

So you can see why I'm apprehensive about striking up conversations on a plane. My track record hasn't been so good. It is much easier for me to stand before a group of 5,000 people and tell my story. Usually I'm telling it to people who agree with me and want to hear it. Most of the time they even pay me to tell it! But often on a plane, it seems I end up sitting next to some person who begins his or her conversation with me by saying, "I don't believe in God" or "Don't you think that all people are worshiping the same God and that all faiths lead to heaven?" What do I do?

I guess it's a question that has followed me all my life, and it is probably a question most committed Christians face: How do I share my faith without sounding like a complete nerd? I hope you've asked yourself this question. If you have, it means that you are taking your faith seriously. When you love Jesus Christ and know His love, you can't help but want to tell people about Him. He even tells us that He expects us to tell others about Him. He wants everyone to know Him. Sharing our faith comes with the territory, but that doesn't mean it's always easy.

Another excuse I give for not wanting to sit next to other people on a plane is that I usually do most of my reading on planes. It is really frustrating to be in the middle of a book and have someone whom you know you'll never see again ask you, "Who do you think will win the Super Bowl this year?" I always feel like a kid in school when someone asks me a question like that. Although I know that there is no right or wrong answer, I feel as if I have to come up with the right one nevertheless. I guess I'm afraid, too, that whatever answer I come up with will be ridiculed. That happened to me one time. A guy asked, "Who do you think will win the Super Bowl this year?" I put down my book, thought a moment, and ventured my guess, "I think Miami has a good chance."

"Miami! No way! They'll be lucky to make the play-offs!" The guy was obviously an avid football fan.

I tried to apologize and explain that I really didn't follow football all that closely. I was just starting to pick up my book to resume reading when he started to lecture me on the strengths and weaknesses of all the teams he considered major contenders for the Super Bowl crown. I listened politely, burning inside, wishing I had the nerve to say, "I really want to read my book," but figuring that that would be rude. I listened, periodically nodding my head as if I really cared. The man went on for what seemed like an hour. When I thought that he was winding down, I quickly picked up my book and started to read again. Even though I tried to look engrossed, he had to ask just one more question, "What do you do for a living?"

There it was. That question. I considered my options. "Well, I'm on a leave of absence from my teaching position and I am traveling and speaking."

"What are you speaking about?"

"Oh, all different kinds of things."

"Like what?"

"Well, I usually share my life story and tell about how teachers and other adults helped mold and shape my life."

He looked at me. "Are you famous or something?"

"No," I chuckled, "I'm not famous."

He continued, "Then forgive me for asking, but why would anyone want to listen to you?"

"I try to talk about things of the heart—important things."

"Like what?" He was curious.

I knew that God was opening the door, but I sensed that this guy, whose conversation had been peppered with profanity, probably would mock me if I told him about Jesus. But, on the other hand, maybe he would leave me alone and I could get back to my book. I decided to answer his question, "I often talk about how Jesus Christ transformed my life."

He jumped at me, "You, religious?" He didn't give me a chance to answer before he continued, "I believe in God, but I don't get carried away with it. I haven't been to church for years."

"I don't consider myself to be 'religious' either," I said. "I consider Christianity a relationship with God, and not a religion."

"Like I said, I haven't been to church for years—ever since my wife died." He said it matter of factly, but something in his eyes spoke more than his words. I could tell that this guy was lonely and had a wounded heart.

"Sorry to hear about your wife," I said and meant it.

"Yeah, cancer. Forty-two years old." He paused for a moment. "Well, we all got to go some time." He tried to pass it off with a laugh.

"Forty-two is awfully young to die," I said. "You must miss her very much."

I must have hit a nerve because his face flushed, and I thought he was going to cry. "Yeah, I do," was his reply.

"When my parents died, I realized how much God really loves me and how much strength and peace He really has to give me. I don't think I could have endured without my faith in God." I hoped that I hadn't come on too fast.

I looked at him, now very quiet. "Do you believe that you'll be with your wife again someday?"

"You mean like heaven?" Perhaps there was just a note of sarcasm in his voice.

"Yeah, I mean heaven. Do you believe that there is a heaven and a hell?"

"Well, if there is a heaven, my wife is there. She was a saint." His eyes were obviously red now.

"Do you remember an old Peggy Lee song?" I asked. It goes, "Is this all there is, my friend? Is this all there is? If this is all there is, then let's break out the booze and have a ball."

"Yeah, I like that song," he said.

"I can't for one minute believe that this is all there is. I believe there is a heaven and a hell, and I believe that because of what Jesus has done I'll see my parents again some day."

"I believe hell is right here on this earth," the man replied. His tone of voice indicated that this was a well-worn belief of his.

"I believe in the Bible," I said.

"The Bible is full of contradictions," he said.

"Oh, like what?" I asked.

"I don't know, but it contradicts itself all the time."

"You know what hit me one day?" I didn't really expect him to answer so I continued, "It hit me that Jesus either was who He said He was or He was a fake or mentally ill or completely deluded. And it hit me: If Jesus is who He said He is, then I want to follow Him completely."

This time he seemed uncomfortable and tried to change the subject. "Well, like I've told you several times, I'm not religious." Now he was trying to shut me off.

By this time I had forgotten my book. God had opened a window of opportunity for me to present the Gospel, the Good News, to this man, and I wasn't finished yet. I knew that I had to win his attention again. I knew, too, that it was important that I didn't sound too "preachy" or set myself up as "holier than thou." Now I wasn't going to let the conversation die. "My mom had stomach cancer. What kind of cancer did your wife have?" I asked.

"Ovarian cancer," he said, suddenly losing all the combativeness that had been in his voice just a few minutes earlier.

I decided to raise one of the tough questions before he did, "My mom was only 59 when she died. I know that is almost 20 years older than your wife was when she died, but I still think it's too early to die. I got really mad at God and shook my fist at Him and asked Him why."

He almost smiled. "What did God say?"

"It felt like He just wrapped His arms around me as I pounded on His chest and told me that He understood. Well, I didn't understand. . . ."

He was curious again, "So, what did you do?"

"I trusted Him."

The plane shook as it hit some turbulence, and the pilot told us all to fasten our seat belts. "That's God trying to get our attention," I joked. "He's shaking His fist back at me!"

That time he did smile.

We talked some more. I told him that the Bible points to Jesus Christ as our Savior and shows us the blessings of living in a close relationship with Him. I always love telling people about the Jesus of the Bible. He is dynamic. He offers everything the world is looking for, every-thing the world needs. Sometimes God almost has to hit me over the head to show me that He is opening up a chance for me to witness, but there are times when I do seek opportunities to share my faith!

I tried witnessing off and on through high school. Throughout junior and senior high school I wore buttons that said things like this: "God is not dead; I just talked to Him this morning" and "Jesus cares." My car carried a bumper sticker that read "Honk if you love Jesus!" I realize now that many people consid-ered me to be a nerd, although I never thought of myself as one.

I'll never forget my first experience in door-to-door evangelism. It came at a time when I was at the height of my bumper-sticker period. Faith Lutheran Church in Staples hosted a training session for anyone in the community who was interested. We were to pair up with someone else, go door to door, and see if we could get ourselves invited into homes to pre-sent the Gospel. If extended an invitation to enter a house, we were to find out whether or not the person or people had a church home. Then, depending on their answer, we were to tactfully ask them about their relationship with Jesus Christ.

If we sensed that our host or hosts did not have a commitment to Christ we were to present a little pamphlet called "The ABCs of Life." The ABCs presented the Gospel in a plain and simple fashion: (A) God loves you and wants you to know abundant and eternal life. (B) You are sinful by nature and by choice, and this sin separates you from God. (C) Jesus Christ is God's provision for your sin. He offers you the free gifts of eternal life and forgiveness of sins.

I was paired with Mrs. Floistad, the Lutheran minister's wife. We were both quite nervous as we went out to knock on doors. We were both confident, however, that we couldn't screw up as badly as one guy did. One of our trainers told us that the pastor of Christ the King Lutheran Church went out one day to go door to door. He must have been even more nervous than Mrs. Floistad and I were. At the first house the lady was slow in answering his knock. When she finally did, he stepped back as she opened the door. He fell off the step and into a hedge. Quickly standing and trying to regain his composure, he brushed himself off and said, "Hi, I'm Christ the King!"

Without missing a beat, the lady who answered the door said, "Come on in; I've been expecting you."

Mrs. Floistad and I didn't have that kind of experience. We did, however, have the opportunity to present the ABCs to several people. One lady prayed with us about her faith in Jesus. We put her name on a list so that appropriate follow-up could be made and so she would receive help finding good church fellowship. It was a great experience.

I have done some door-to-door evangelism since, but most of my evangelistic endeavors have been in front of large groups of people. My experience on the plane that day, however, with the man whose wife had died of cancer reminded me that most evangelism occurs one-to-one when we are not necessarily expecting it.

Paul told the Corinthians that their lives were "letters." He told them that everybody was reading their letters. He said that the Holy Spirit writes our letters for us on the tablets of peoples' hearts (2 Corinthians 3:2–3). Think of it! I often wonder what other people "read" when they read the letter of my life. There is no doubt about it: Essential to the effectiveness of our witnessing is the way we live.

I know that many of the students I've taught have asked the same question I have: "How do I share my faith without sounding like a nerd?" I've discovered some things about sharing my faith that seem to work for me. The first thing I think is essential is to know for sure what your faith is. You have to know what you believe and why you believe it, but don't worry about not having all the answers. If in the process of sharing your faith, someone asks you a question that stumps you that's good. The Holy Spirit will help your faith grow in the areas where you are challenged.

I remember when I began to venture out and share my faith. Fellow students asked me some really tough questions. Questions like these:

"What does the Bible have to say about dinosaurs?"

"If God can do anything, can He make a mountain so big He can't move it?"

"Where did God come from?"

"How could someone have always been here? Doesn't everything have to have a beginning?"

"What about all the people in the world who've never heard about God? What's going to happen to them?"

"If you believe in heaven and hell, tell me where they are located."

"How big would Noah's ark have to have been to get two of every kind of animal in it?"

These were only a few of the questions I regularly encountered. Today whenever I encounter a question I don't have a ready answer for, I make a mental note and try to find the answer in God's Word before I have an opportunity to witness again. That's one of the ways my faith grows. Sometimes I just have to admit that I don't have all the answers and that no one does. If we had all the answers, then we'd be God. It may sound corny, but much of faith boils down to having faith!

I also try to avoid arguing about things like Noah's ark. Instead, I try to focus on Jesus Christ and what He has done for me. I've discovered that there is no one who can argue with me when I share about my personal experiences with Jesus. People will argue with me about creation and evolution and the flood and miracles recorded in the Bible, but when I share my story about how Jesus has changed my life and given me real strength, no one can argue with me because they can't tell me I'm wrong!

If I sense that God is opening a window for me to share, I ask Him for the right words to say and for the guidance of the Holy Spirit. I've witnessed what has happened when the Holy Spirit touches someone. I've seen hardened hearts softened and closed minds opened. If you feel that God is leading you to share your faith with someone, don't forget to pray and ask for His guidance!

I always like to begin any sharing time with others by talking about something that we have in common: sports, music, something we are doing together, etc. Let the other person see that you are just a regular person too. It helps to show a genuine interest. Ask questions. Listen well when the other person speaks. Don't be too busy figuring out the next thing you're going to say. When you listen well and concentrate on the person to whom you are speaking, you validate that person's feelings and show that you are sincere. God will help you with the next thing you are going to say. Trust Him.

In my early days of witnessing I felt compelled to point out every wrong belief I heard someone express. Usually that only led to arguments. I've discovered that I can say I don't agree with someone without directly telling them so. The way I do this is to, once again, simply tell my story. For instance, if someone says, "I don't believe that God really cares," I'm setting myself up for an argument if I say, "Oh, but I believe He does." It's much more effective to share my own personal experience like this:

"I hear you. It can seem like God is a million miles away sometimes. I used to feel that He was way up there and didn't really care. What I discovered was that it wasn't God who was far away from me, but that it was me who was far away from God. Once God's Holy Spirit helped me listen to God's promises and do things His way, I discovered just how much He really did care."

One of the most thrilling opportunities I have as a Christian is the opportunity to pray with someone who desires to know Jesus Christ as their best friend, their Lord, and their Savior. And what about being a nerd? Try following these steps:

1. Know what you believe and why you believe it.
2. Don't worry about not having all the answers, and admit that you don't.
3. Pray and ask God for the guidance of the Holy Spirit.
4. Show a genuine interest in the people to whom you are speaking. Listen well. Establish common ground. Validate their feelings and show an appreciation for where they are spiritually.
5. Avoid judging or condemning. Instead, stick to your story. No one can argue with you when you share what has happened to you as a result of your personal walk with Christ.
6. Take the opportunity to ask them to pray with you about their relationship with God.

If you try an approach like this, you will come across in a sincere fashion and, with the Holy Spirit's help, almost anyone will listen to you without thinking that you are a jerk.

One other point: Don't be discouraged if you don't seem to get anywhere with your witnessing. Trust God. The Bible teaches us that some people plant the seeds, other people water them, and God causes them to grow (1 Corinthians 3:6–7).

One final word: Don't be too concerned about being a nerd. The Bible also teaches that we shouldn't be too concerned with what others think about us. Instead, we should be most concerned with what God thinks about us. Expect persecution and ridicule for sharing your faith. It comes with the territory. Paul asked these questions: "Am I now trying to win the approval of men, or of God? Or am I trying to please men? If I were still trying to please men, I would not be a servant of Christ" (Galatians 1:10). Paul also said, "I am not ashamed of the gospel, because it is the power of God for the salvation of everyone who believes" (Romans 1:16).

Remember the man on the plane? The flight attendant announced that we were making our final approach into the airport. In the course of our conversation about who was likely to win the Super Bowl, cancer, the Bible, and how God is able to fill longing hearts, my fellow traveler and I had eventually exchanged names. Ray looked at me. "It's been good talking with you," he said.

"I've really enjoyed talking with you, too, Ray. I want you know that I'll be praying for you. I hope you find a good church. God has been good to me. He's got lots of blessings to give you too."

"Thanks," he said, "I appreciate that."

I took my book that I'd been trying to read and tucked it into the bag that I slid under the seat in front of me. God hadn't wanted me to read that day; He wanted me to plant some seeds.

Unwanted Visits

*What Is Sexual Abuse and
What Do You Do about It?*

I remember. I was in world literature class. We were reading *Cyrano de Bergerac*, and I was reading the part of Cyrano. It was a role I tackled with great enthusiasm. Poor Cyrano. He had such a heart and such a soul, and yet Roxane, the subject of his affection, was unaware of his deep love for her. And he dared not tell her lest she think him insane. He wondered who could possibly love a man with such a grotesque nose?

I had assigned various parts from the play to some of the students in the class, and we were reading it aloud when we heard a knock on the classroom door. Without missing a beat, I walked to the door and opened it. There stood Shelly. She was supposed to have been in the class.

ABUSE

144

"Mr. Doud," she said, "can I talk to you for a few minutes?" Tears streamed down her face.

"Mark, will you read Cyrano's part for me, please?" As much as I dislike interruptions in my classes, I knew that something was very wrong with Shelly or she wouldn't have asked to talk. I wondered why she wasn't in class. And why the tears? The last few weeks I had noticed how Shelly's disposition had changed and how her performance in class had declined. A girl with a normally bubbly personality, I hadn't seen much of Shelly's smile in the last month.

I shut the door behind me. "Shelly, what's wrong?"

"It's my stepfather," she said, "he's been visiting my room."

I wondered why she had chosen me to share her secret. I stood in shock for a moment as her tears turned to sobs. I put my hand on her shoulder, wondering how much trust she could have for any man. Yet I realized that she must have trusted me to tell me what she did. Before I said anything, she spoke again, "I told my mom about it, but she told me not to tell anyone. She said that she would 'talk to him about it.' " More tears.

I knew that in cases of sexual abuse, family members often attempt to cover up what is happening. I asked Shelly to go to the guidance office with me.

"If I tell anyone, my mother will kill me," she said. "My stepfather will get in trouble, and it will deotroy our whole family "

"Shelly, your stepfather made a decision to destroy your family when he abused you."

Shelly was crying almost uncontrollably now. "I can't tell anyone," she said.

"I have to," I said. Legally, I had a responsibility to report any physical or sexual abuse.

"I trusted you," she said.

"Then trust me to do what is best, Shelly."

"Oh, my mother is going to kill me."

"She might not understand right now, but someday she will."

I walked Shelly to the guidance office where I explained the situation to her counselor. I left Shelly with him and returned to my class.

My students were still faithfully reading from *Cyrano,* but I had a difficult time thinking of anything except Shelly.

I have known many victims of sexual abuse. Most were abused as young children. Some, like Shelly, were abused teenagers. In every case I've known, the effects are the same. The victim is left with a deep sense of shame and guilt. Somehow, victims believe that they are to blame for what has happened.

What constitutes sexual abuse of a child (or young person)? Simply put, if anyone is using a child in any way so as to receive sexual stimulation, that is sexual child abuse. It may include such things as inappropriate touching, engaging in a sexual act with a child, forcing a child to look at pornography or participate in its production, or making a child watch an adult or adults have sex or masturbate. An important point: Sexual abuse does not always involve touching a child. Many children are harmed emotionally as a result of exhibitionists who have exposed themselves. Incest means that the abuse is perpetrated by another family member. Recent reports suggest that as many as one in four girls may be incest victims.

Recently we've heard much news concerning sexual abuse. Popular entertainment personalities have shared their stories. The news has carried numerous stories about clergy and other professionals who have abused children. Many abused children so deeply repress the pain of the abuse that they do not remember it until they are adults.

One friend shared with me how she had been abused by an uncle. She was only three or four years old at the time, and she wasn't sure exactly what had happened. He told her not to tell her mother because her mother would spank her if she found out what she had done. She didn't tell. Instead, she hid the secret deep inside of her where it remained until she was nearly 40. Then, after frequent headaches and deep depression, she sought counseling. During the counseling sessions, her painful past surfaced.

Through counseling, she discovered that the sexual abuse had caused deep psychological problems. She viewed sex as something dirty and shameful, and she had never enjoyed making love with her husband. This had caused problems in her marriage. During counseling, she discovered that she had probably been depressed ever since she had been abused. She had grown up not really knowing what it feels like to be normal and happy. She thought everyone felt like she did. She found it difficult to trust anyone, especially men. Her pain also caused her to use food as an anesthetic. She ate more and more, without even realizing why she was eating. Her obesity affected her sense of self-worth. The worse she felt about herself, the more she ate. The more she ate, the worse she felt. It was a vicious cycle of addiction.

My friend's situation was complicated by the fact that the uncle who abused her was still alive. She saw him occasionally at family gatherings. Part of her recovery involved confronting him. She wondered if anyone would believe her, and she feared that the confrontation would divide her family.

Sometimes the victim of sexual abuse blames God, wondering how God could possibly have allowed it to happen. Feelings of distrust are directed at God as well.

If the abuse is committed by a member of the same sex, the victim may suffer even more shame and may struggle with sexual identity issues.

My friend's situation is not uncommon. Often the abuse is perpetrated by a trusted adult, or even a loved one. The abuser may be a professional person whom no one would ever suspect of abusing children. When the abuse occurs, childhood security is destroyed. The victim finds ways to survive the pain. In later life, the victim will often abuse an addictive agent of some kind: food, drugs, alcohol, work, perfectionism, sex, etc. The victim often hides behind thick walls of repression and denial. Admitting what has happened is just too painful. But what has happened is like a cancer inside the body. It must be removed.

The first step on the road to wellness is for the victim to acknowledge and seek help from an experienced therapist who supports and acknowledges her or his Spirit-given faith in Jesus. Such a therapist can lead the victim down the road of recovery. Christ specializes in giving people whole new lives. His love, forgiveness, and understanding is needed so that healing can take place.

My friend did confront her uncle, but she said that she would have never been able to do so without the strength God had given her. Eventually, because of the grace and the love of God within her, she forgave her uncle and let go of her resentment.

A well-known celebrity shared how she had been sexually abused by a family member when she was very young. After her confession, I heard someone sarcastically comment, "Why don't these people just get on with their lives and quit living in the past?" Many people seem to have this attitude. They don't understand that there is a large crack in the foundation of the abused person's life. In order to "get on with life," it is necessary to go back and tear up the old foundation and replace it with a new one. And there is no better foundation than the love of Jesus.

If you have been sexually abused or think you may have been, do not keep your abuse a secret. The sooner you receive help, the sooner the cancer can be removed. It is frightening to tell someone that you've been abused, but the alternative is even more frightening—a life without the ability to enjoy the love and freedom from shame that Christ gives us so freely.

If a friend tells you that she or he has been abused, encourage your friend to seek help immediately. If the abuse is happening now, seek the guidance of your parents, a pastor, a teacher, or a guidance counselor. It is vital that any recent incident or suspected incident be reported to legal authorities. My experience has shown that after a report is made, everything is done to protect and care for the victim and to safeguard his or her best interest. Another important reason why abuse should be reported is that people who abuse children sexually seldom only abuse once. They abuse again and again. They must be stopped.

Jesus Christ specializes in giving new life. He is able to give us new minds, and He provides us with a new way of thinking. He puts hope back in our hopeless eyes, and He teaches us to trust Him.

Jesus has tremendous compassion for the victims of sexual abuse. He calls us to follow His example. We must walk beside them and demonstrate His love and understanding.

The Wandering Star

If God Is Love,
  Why Is There So Much Pain
    and Suffering in the World?

Before the day was over, I think I ate about 21 pieces of fried chicken. I lost the exact count somewhere around 15 pieces because I was distracted. I was trying to eat chicken and play softball at the same time.

Now before you think of me as a glutton (which I guess I definitely was), I had best explain the situation to you. I was at a party for the cast and crew of *Paint Your Wagon*, the musical our high school choir had just finished performing. I had the lead role in the show. I was Ben Rumson, the part made famous by Lee Marvin in the movie. In the stage version of the show, Ben sings two well-known songs, "They Call the Wind Maria" and "I Was Born under a Wandering Star." At the cast party, it seems that my wandering star kept leading me to the buckets of chicken.

153

In fairness to myself, I must explain to you that I was a growing boy with an appetite that was hard to appease and I had just finished the final performance of the show. I had expended lots of energy. Singing and acting burns thousands of calories, you know. And now I was playing softball and running around the bases and yelling. Being athletic like that really burns up calories. So whenever I wasn't out in the field or up to bat, you could find me at the chicken buckets. Thankfully Mr. Carlson, our choir director, had supplied plenty of chicken, and there was more than enough for everyone to eat their fill.

I think I probably ate more chicken than anybody else, but Brian ate quite a few pieces too. Brian and I had become pretty good friends during all the weeks of practicing *Paint Your Wagon.* Brian loved to joke, and his sharp wit started the entire cast laughing many times. It was obvious that Brian was very intelligent, and more than once I wished I had his brains.

"How many pieces have you had, Guy?" Brian asked, as we both met by the buckets of chicken that sat on the picnic table in Mr. Carlson's backyard.

"I don't know for sure, but I think this is my 15th," I said, rather proud of my accomplishment.

"So, you're just getting started."

I laughed.

"What are you going to do after you graduate?" Brian asked. He was a junior, so I knew he had another year to put in at Staples High School.

I was a senior, and in only a month I would be finishing my years as a high school student. A lot of people had asked me that question lately.

"I'm going to go to the Community College in Brainerd," I said. "I'm either going to be a teacher or a preacher or an actor."

"It's good to keep your options open," Brian said, rather sardonically.

"I'm really going to miss choir next year," I said, reaching for another piece of chicken.

"You'll survive, I'm sure, and I bet you'll never go hungry." Characteristically Brian. He was such a stoic, and I wondered if he ever showed any emotion.

A month later at the graduation ceremony in the high school gymnasium, I cried a river of tears as I sang "The Halls of Ivy" along with the other seniors in the choir. After the ceremony, everybody was hugging everybody else. I stood outside the choir room near the gymnasium, and tears continued to flow as fellow students congratulated me and each other. There were many wishes of good luck and more questions about what the future held. As I hugged and thanked people, I knew that I would never see some of these friends again.

"You behave yourself now, Guy, and be sure to get plenty to eat." It was Brian, and he gave me a great big hug, "Take care of yourself man. I'm going to miss you."

Someday when I get to heaven I have lots of questions for God. One of those questions is why He made me the way He did. As I sit here at my word processor and type this story about Brian, tears are pouring down my cheeks, just like they did that day of my high school graduation. Why did God make me like this? Why can't I be more stoic like many other men? Why do I cry over some television commercials or as I look at my children's baby pictures. Why?

"Thank you, Brian," I said, blubbering some more as I hugged him back. "You behave yourself too."

The next time I saw Brian, a little over a year later, he was in a casket.

I'm sorry for telling you so bluntly, but that's how I received the news too. "Brian died," the caller said and then asked if I would be willing to do the eulogy at his funeral. Of course I was filled with a multitude of feelings—first shock, then disbelief, then wonder, then selfish feelings about how it would affect me, then feelings of intense anger. How could

God let this happen? Brian was only eighteen. Eighteen!

The summer of his senior year Brian had gotten a job working for the railroad replacing railroad ties and laying new track. I think they call it working on the chain gang. It was a very hot Minnesota summer day. Although Minnesota is known for its cold, Arctic winters, summer temperatures do reach the hundreds occasionally. It was as hot as Minnesota ever gets the day that Brian died.

The way I heard the story, Brian was perspiring profusely and asked his foreman if he could rest. The foreman was less than sympathetic and forced Brain to continue working. A few moments later, Brian collapsed and died of heat exhaustion. I never knew if the story was completely true, but I hated the foreman nonetheless. I blamed him for Brian's death, and I blamed God.

When I was a sophomore in high school my grandmother died. We were very close, and I took her death very hard. When I was a junior in high school my grandfather, Guy James Rice, died. I took his death even harder. I had been named after Grandpa. He had been that special person to me who seemed to understand me when no one else in the world did. But my grandparents were both almost 90 when they died. I knew that it was unrealistic to expect people to live forever, but what about Brian? He was only eighteen.

As a Christian I knew that Christ had conquered death. I knew that Brian was very much alive and that he was with Jesus. I knew, too, as with my grandparents, that I would see Brian again someday. Yet at the time of Brian's death I still felt that life wasn't fair.

Brian didn't live long enough to discover that I became a teacher and a preacher and an actor. One experience I had as a teacher demonstrated dramatically to me how unfair life really is. A student from our high school, Kent Soderman, whose story is told in my film and book *Molder of Dreams* was a patient at Children's Hospital in Minneapolis where he was being treated for a cancerous brain tumor. I had taken a bus load of my student council students to the Minnesota state capital for the day. On the way back to Brainerd we stopped at Children's Hospital to visit Kent. Since he was very susceptible to any virus, only two people at a time could visit with him and they had to wear masks over their mouths. The rest of the students waited outside his room which was right across from the nurses' desk.

I'll never forget the nurse who sat at the desk and held the most beautiful little girl on her lap. The girl was totally bald, but you hardly noticed the baldness because she had such

158

big blue eyes and such an infectious smile. She laughed as the nurse played patty cake with her. One student asked, "What's wrong with her?"

"She has leukemia, but we're doing all we can to make her better."

"How old is she?" another student asked.

"We just had a birthday party for her the other day," the nurse answered. "She just turned three."

Three, I thought. That's my son Seth's age. Three. It isn't fair.

On the bus on the way home, one of my students, Amy, came up to me. I knew that Amy was actively involved in her church youth group and was a committed Christian.

"I can't get over all those sick children," she said, "and Julie said a lot of them only have a short time to live." It sounded as if she was asking me if I thought Julie was right.

"Many of them do only have a short time to live," I said, "but treatment has come a long way and many of them will get better."

"It doesn't seem fair," she said, as though she expected me to disagree with her.

"It isn't," I said. "It's not fair at all."

"Then why does God allow it?" She sounded angry.

"You know, everyone thinks that is such a hard question to answer, but I think the answer is really quite simple."

"What's the answer?"

"Most of the pain and suffering in the world is the result of sin and the sinful decisions that we as people have made. It is unfair that little babies have to suffer because of decisions made by someone else, but if God were to take away all the pain and all the suffering, He would have to take away our freedom to make choices. If He did that we would no longer be human. We would be robots. We would be incapable of love."

Amy thought for a moment and then said, "I don't see how Kent or those other kids are sick because of the decisions made by someone else."

"It is hard to understand that. That's why I agree that it isn't fair, but God never intended for there to be any pain or suffering in the world. He gave Adam and Eve a perfect world and told them that they could do whatever they wanted—with one exception." I stopped and looked at Amy.

"I know," she said, "they weren't supposed to eat of the tree."

"Do you know what that tree was called?" I asked.

"The tree of knowledge," she answered.

"Knowledge of what?" I asked.

"I don't remember," she admitted.

"It was the tree of the knowledge of good and evil."

"So what was so bad about eating from that tree?" Amy asked, sounding rather perplexed.

"Think about it. Good and evil. Before they ate of the fruit of that tree, everything was good. They knew no evil. They ran around the garden unclothed, unashamed."

"But I still don't understand why God didn't want them to eat of that tree."

"Yeah, that's the bottom line. What God was basically saying was this: 'You can do whatever you want to do, but please let me be God. Don't you try to be God. Obey Me and let Me be God.' "

"I've never heard it explained that way before," Amy said. "That makes sense. But why did God allow the serpent to tempt Adam and Eve in the first place?"

"The serpent was the devil. The Bible tells us that the devil uses all kinds of disguises. Sometimes he even "masquerades as an angel of light" (2 Corinthians 11:14). We know that he is a fallen angel. It appears that God gives his angels freedom and that the devil has freedom, too, although God has curtailed his freedom." I had told Amy at the beginning of our conversation that I thought the answer was pretty simple. I imagined that she probably was wondering by now what I considered a complicated answer to be!

"I think the world would have been a lot better off if God had not—and would not—allow the devil to tempt people," Amy said after thinking for a moment.

"I do too, Amy, but love can't be forced or demanded. The Holy Spirit helps us see the great love God gives us in Jesus. But people can still choose to ignore God."

There was a moment of silence as we bounced along in the big, orange monster. It was Amy who broke the silence, "So what Adam and Eve chose to do has affected the world ever since."

"Yeah, it has. The decision they made brought death into the world."

"That's what seems unfair," Amy said.

"You know, I bet if we'd been in Adam and Eve's shoes we probably would have done the same thing. And you and I are making decisions right now that will cause consequences for people years from now."

"Like what?" Amy asked.

"Look out the window," I said. "Less than a hundred years ago you could have traveled this country and encountered numerous wild animals that now are almost extinct. We could have stopped at the river there and we could have drunk freely from its waters. Now many of the rivers are so polluted that we can't even eat fish that we catch in them. You drive your car and I drive mine, and the ozone continues to be depleted—a problem that will be even more threatening for your children than it is for mine." I stopped and looked at Amy. "Do you want me to go on?"

"I get your point," she said, but she sounded discouraged.

I wanted to tell her that I believed that the effects of sin are accumulative too. When I was a teenager, people rarely lived together and marriage was still fashionable. Divorce was a rarity. If you called someone "gay" it meant that they were happy. Elvis Presley gyrating his hips was about as shocking as rock music ever got. I thought of the rock group who had attracted media attention recently when they had performed a graphic sexual act on stage and the rock group whose lead singer attributed his success to Satan during a music awards program on MTV. What kind of world will my grandchildren inherit? And who is to blame?

"But there is good news, Amy," I said.

"What's that, Mr. Doud?" Amy asked.

"Life is unfair, but God is good. That's why He sent Jesus."

I watched Amy's face soften and her eyes moisten. She spoke, "I never knew how much Jesus could really help me until my parents got divorced a couple of years ago. At first, I even wanted to blame God for allowing them to get divorced, but then I realized that it wasn't His fault. And then I realized that He was always there for me."

"And He always will be, Amy. And He's there for Kent, too, and for that little girl you saw the nurse holding in her lap."

I thought of the wandering star that stopped over an obscure little village called Bethlehem over two thousand years ago. Its light shone in a manger where lay the light and the hope of the world. Born to common parents, this baby grew to understand better than anyone else ever has just how unfair life is. He never committed any crime or any sin, and yet He was punished for the sins of all humanity. He showed love to those who hated Him and wanted to put Him to death. Some of His most trusted friends betrayed him. If anyone can possibly understand how unfair life is, He can. If anyone can possibly understand your feelings of rejection, He can.

Each year around the middle of May I make a trip to Staples, my hometown. I plant flowers there at the graves of my great grandparents, my grandparents, and my mother and father. After my task is done, I spend some time just walking through the rest of the cemetery. I stop at lots of graves and remember. One grave I always visit is Brian's. The next time I stop at Brian's grave, I'm going to sing a song. And I know that I can sing it because of the wandering star and Bethlehem and who it was who lay there in that manger. The song is going to go like this:

When I get to heaven,
Don't tie me to a tree,
Because I've got lots of folks
That I really need to see.

He Didn't Read the *Inferno* but He Found One

I'm Struggling in School. Any Suggestions?

Kyle was one of the "lucky" ones. School always came easily for him. As his teacher, I was always amazed at how well he could do with seemingly little effort. In addition to his good grades, mostly A's and B's, he managed to participate in three different sports, sing in the choir, serve on the student council and in the senior class cabinet, and hold down a part-time job at Wendy's. I was impressed.

I had Kyle in a number of my advanced English classes. I couldn't understand where he found the time to read Dante's *Inferno* and *Beowulf* when he was making tackles out on the gridiron or flipping burgers at Wendy's. He seemed to have an uncanny ability to do well on tests—even essay tests—despite the fact I doubted he had read the material. It seemed unfair because many students read all of their assignments and spent many hours studying and were just barely able to survive.

When I demanded more of Kyle, he was the one who howled "unfair" and wondered why I was requiring more of him than I did my other students. He had a point, but I answered him, "To those whom much has been given, much is expected."

I doubted that Kyle was going to be able to breeze through college as he had high school. I was right. Because of his good grades and impressive school activity record, Kyle was accepted at a college with a strong academic reputation. Several weeks into his freshman year I saw Kyle at the homecoming game.

"How is college going, Kyle?" I asked.

"It sure is different from high school," he said.

"What do you mean, different?" I asked.

"I can't believe how much the profs expect you to study each night, and I never really learned how to study in high school. I'm struggling to keep my head above water."

I detected true concern and anxiety in Kyle's voice. I asked, "How were you able to get through high school without having to study?"

"I don't know," was his honest answer. "I guess things just came easily for me."

I saw Kyle again a couple of months later. He had dropped out of the college he was attending after the first quarter and had decided to take a few semesters off to save up some money. His grades for the first semester of his freshman year were mostly C's, D's, and no-credits. When he applied to attend another college, he was surprised to discover that it was difficult getting accepted. Even though he was accepted and placed on academic probation, none of the few credits he had earned transferred. He was back at square one, and this time he had to maintain his grade point average to remain in school. This time Kyle told me, "I sure wish I had learned how to study. College is worse than the *Inferno*, Mr. Doud."

I've known lots of students like Kyle. Many go through junior and senior high school not taking their studies very seriously. Many receive a rude awakening when they reach college. You probably expect someone like me, a high school teacher, to tell you to study hard and do your best in school. But the reason I give you that advice may be different than you expect. Also, I feel I have an obligation, if I tell you to study hard, to also give you some tips on how to do it.

Why should you study? There are the obvious reasons, of course. You want to graduate! If you don't, you may face the wrath of your teachers and your parents! Then there are a few reasons you may not have considered: God asks you to always do your best so that your life as a Christian brings glory to Him. Your being in school is no accident. I believe it is part of God's will for you. I think you are safe in assuming that school is where God wants you to be and God will help you to give it all you've got.

I had a friend in college named Brad. Brad was intent on knowing God's will for his life. That sounds like an admirable quality until you hear more about Brad. Every morning Brad would get out of bed and start his day by asking, "What do you want me to do today, God?" According to Brad, God usually told him to go witness to students in the student center.

"Does God ever tell you to go to class," I asked.

"Seldom," answered Brad.

"I'm not sure you're really hearing God's voice," I said.

Brad declared me a heretic and continued to begin each day by asking God what he should do that day. I would often see Brad at a table in the student center, actively engaged in dialog with someone who seemed to want to study. I saw him there, that is, until he finally dropped out of college.

I walked by Brad's room as he packed to move out. I knocked and he invited me in. "God wants me to leave college," he said. "My poor grades are a sign."

I wondered if it would do any good if I told him that the only thing his poor grades were a sign of were poor study habits. I figured not. I couldn't believe that Brad had enrolled in college, paid thousands of dollars in tuition fees, and then believed that God didn't want him to do his studies.

Let me say it again: If you are in school, more than likely you are there because it is where God wants you right now. Enjoy your school years and honor God in all your studies and activities.

I love students like Jill. She came into my high school classroom somewhat apprehensively. Her voice was tentative when she asked, "Mr. Doud, can I talk with you for a few moments?"

"Sure, Jill," I said.

"Mr. Doud, no matter how hard I study for your tests I don't do very well." She sounded completely frustrated.

Jill was in my world literature class where most of the tests were essay tests. Jill was flirting with a failing grade because she seemed unable to write essay answers that adequately answered the questions.

She continued, "I'm spending all my time studying for your class. It's affecting my grades in my other classes. Even though I study so much for your class, it doesn't seem to do any good. What can I do?"

I asked Jill a series of questions about the subject matter, and it was obvious to me that she had a good understanding of the material. Her weakness was that she didn't know how to organize her knowledge in an essay. She didn't understand proper essay form.

Jill and I sat at a table. I wrote out a sample essay question and, step by step, I showed her how to answer it. Soon Jill was offering suggestions, and I could see things beginning to click for her. I told her that she could take the tests that she had failed over again if she desired. She anxiously jumped at the offer, and when she did retake them, I was amazed at how much she had improved.

Jill, whether she realized it or not, had followed one of the cardinal rules for doing well in school: She asked for help. In all my years of teaching, I have never had a student fail a course who was sincerely interested in doing well and asked for extra help. On the other hand, I am amazed by those students who stand on the ledge of failure and never reach for anything to keep them from falling off. Success in school begins with your attitude. Do you want to do well or are you indifferent? If you are a Christian and remember all that

Christ has done for us, indifference really isn't an option.

Another positive factor Jill had going for her, besides her good attitude, was her good attendance. Success in school is directly related to your attendance. It is important that you go to class each day, expecting to be involved and prepared to learn. Try this sometime. When you come to class, greet your teacher and make some positive comment about the assignment you did the night before. (No, that's not brown-nosing! And even if it is, teachers love it!) I guarantee that the teacher will be impressed.

Part of being prepared to learn means you come to class with the right attitude, as we've already established, but it also means having the necessary supplies, such as notebooks and books and pens and pencils. If you have an option, sit toward the front of the room. Believe it or not, studies show that students who willingly sit toward the front of the room tend to perform better on tests and receive higher grades.

After helping Jill learn how to answer essay questions, I visited with her about her other study habits.

"I tend to put everything off until the night before it is due," she said.

I chuckled and said, "You and most other students I know. It hasn't been until the last few years that I've actually started to practice my own advice and begin projects as soon as I can."

"What kinds of projects do teachers have?" Jill asked.

"We have to make lessons plans, write tests, correct papers, ugh! It sure is nice doing a little bit each day rather than waiting until the last minute to try and do everything. That's where budgeting my time comes in."

There is another very basic principle concerning success in school: Pray about your studies and make sure that you allow time for the study of God's Word. When I'm budgeting my time, the first thing I schedule is time to read the Bible and to pray. I am a big believer in prayer. I believe God wants us to bring all of our requests to Him. Nothing that concerns us is too insignificant for God. We can't ask God to help us get an A if we haven't done the work to earn one, but we can ask God to help us discipline ourselves, to give us the right attitude, and to give us clear minds.

Every year in our school, as in most high schools across the nation, students take either the ACT or the SAT test. I'm always interested when students share their test results. Many times I am surprised by the results because the students with the highest scores do not necessarily always receive the highest grades. I have a friend who only recently took an IQ test. She had graduated from both high school and college with high honors. She is successful in her profession and is regarded as a very bright lady, which she is. She was absolutely devastated when she discovered that according to her IQ, she is only of average intelligence. I thought the situation humorous, but she didn't. She wanted to retake the IQ test because she figured there must have been a mistake.

I don't know my IQ. I don't want to know it. As far as I'm concerned, I know that God has given me the ability to read and write and think and speak, and with His help, I want to do all those things to the best of my ability. I have seen many students succeed far beyond what their test results would indicate they are capable of. Plain old hard work and determination will often go where mere intelligence can't. God has given you many abilities, too, and this I know: He wants you to use the gifts He has given you to serve Him and to bring honor and glory to His kingdom. Go and serve, with God's blessing.